Forward the the Rifles

Captain David Campbell, M.C.

16 November 1887 - 10 April 1971

6th Royal Irish Rifles

N

First published 2009

Nonsuch Publishing
119 Lower Baggot Street
Dublin 2
Ireland

www.nonsuchireland.com

British Library Cataloguing in Publication Data.
A catalogue record for this book is available from the British Library.

ISBN 978 184588 966 1

Typesetting and origination by The History Press
Printed in Great Britain

Contents

Introduction

David Campbell, my father, was a young man living on the sixty-acre family farm, Crinstown, three miles from Ardee in Co. Louth, in Ireland. His father had died in 1895 while out working in the fields and his mother had brought up the family of eleven on her own. As a boy he had walked those three miles to school in Ardee every day and as a young man he had been a school teacher and had then entered Trinity College, Dublin as a divinity student.

The year was 1914 and the world was about to be engulfed in the Great War, 'The war to end all wars.' Ireland was then part of the United Kingdom of Great Britain and Ireland, and my father, in addition to being a divinity student, was also a member of the Trinity College Officers' Training Corps. So it was that shortly after the outbreak of war he received his orders to report to the Officers' Training School.

Like many Irish soldiers his service took him to Gallipoli, where countless men, many of them Irish men, lost their lives. It was said that after the landings at Gallipoli, black crepe hung from every door in the Coombe in Dublin. He was wounded and was evacuated to England where he recovered. His account of his training and of his service in Gallipoli and later in Salonica is an intensely personal one.

The end of the war brought a period of great change

in the world and particularly in the United Kingdom, where the twenty-six counties of Ireland became an independent sovereign state. After the war my father became a civil engineer. Within his lifetime the flimsy aeroplanes that had flown during the war were replaced by great passenger airliners that could fly over the Atlantic. They needed a major airport in the West of Ireland and he was appointed resident engineer to construct what was to become Shannon Airport.

David Henry Campbell
October 2009

Outbreak of the Great War

4 August 1914

On 4 August 1914, together with the morning paper announcing the outbreak of the war, I received a letter from the Officers' Training Corps, Trinity College, Dublin, inviting me to apply for a commission in the Army. I was twenty-seven years of age.

I had entered Trinity in January 1913 and had joined the OTC in March 1914. So it was that my name was on the books of the War Office; so it came about that I received that fateful letter.

I was working for 'Little Go' at the time, my intention being to enter the Ministry of the Church of Ireland, and having considered the subject for a few days, I consulted the Rector at Ardee. I have forgotten what advice he gave me, but the upshot was that I duly submitted my application for a commission. Having done so and having waited for my excitement to subside I tried to resume my studies. It was not for long.

On 26 August, as I sat at a table on the lawn, swotting Greek, Amelia came in through the garden gate with a letter in her hand which she had just received from the postman. 'Second Lieutenant David Campbell', she announced.

I rose from my seat, took my Greek lexicon in my two hands and kicked it high in the air. 'I'll never open you again', I cried. And I never did resume the study of Greek, though I was just beginning to love the language at the time.

The letter was from the King. 'George by the grace of God', I read, 'of the United Kingdom of Great Britain and Ireland', etc. 'To our Trusty and Well-beloved David Campbell, Greetings'. It was my commission.

When I first applied, I do not think I was inspired by lofty motives. I had no feeling of 'wanting to do my bit' or 'wanting to fight for my country', or 'wanting to serve my King', or any hatred of the Germans or any feeling of patriotism. I think I just wanted to escape from the drab life I was then leading. I had not worked hard enough for my exam. I had spent my time, too much of it, gadding around the county, going to tennis parties, dances and what not, and I was very much afraid I would not pass my 'Little Go'. And so, when the call came, I was ripe for a change and accepted it with joy.

The letter also contained my orders. I was to report forthwith to the Officers' Training School, which had just been established in Trinity. I took my orders literally and at once made preparations to obey them. Indeed I was one of the first to arrive at the school. In a day or two, however, the class was complete.

We were accommodated in tents but had to provide our own camp beds. Tragedy overtook mine on the first night of its service. Two hefty blokes, they must have been sixteen stone apiece, came to visit one of the other occupants of my tent. They had been out on a pub crawl and were pretty well oiled. Mine was the only bed set up at the time and down they sat on it beside me. It was never meant to carry such a load and sure enough something gave under the strain. For ever after, whenever I slept in the bed I could feel those legs sticking into the small of my back.

Most of the 300 or so who attended the school had been

in the OTC for some years and were well acquainted with the rudiments of soldiering. I, however, was a complete novice. When this was discovered, one of the instructors carried me off, stealthily, I thought, to a remote corner of the camp and gave me my first lesson in military drill. 'Right Turn!', 'Left Turn!', 'Quick March!', 'Halt!' I picked it up quickly and soon felt the complete soldier.

In order to clear the books, those who went into the Army had to be discharged from the OTC. When it came to my discharge, it was found that I had not attended any parades. Now, the OTC gets a bonus for every cadet who attends a specified number of parades and passes an Efficiency Test. As I had done neither, I had to be graded as 'Inefficient' and to pay up the amount of the bonus, £5. I was fool enough to pay up, for I am sure I would have been excused had I pleaded inability to pay.

The incident became a legend in the OTC, and at the first Armistice Dinner, held in Trinity on 11 November 1919, the chairman in his speech said, 'And here is Campbell, discharged as "Inefficient" in August 1914, and given a commission, and he comes back as Captain and with his breast covered with medals.'

After one month's training, I had caught up on most of the others and, like them, was passed out and posted to a battalion. Mine was the 6th Royal Irish Rifles, then stationed at Fermoy, Co. Cork. I reported for duty on 4 September and was placed in command of No.2 Platoon.

I felt pretty green as I prepared to face my platoon on my first parade. My batman, an old soldier, a regular, and highly efficient, had me out of bed at 6a.m. that first morning. 'Your bath is ready, Sir', he said. He had carried the water up a couple of flights of stairs and poured it into a bath tub which now stood steaming in the middle of my bedroom floor. I hadn't the courage to tell him I didn't want a bath just then. And so it was for many a long day. He took command, saw that I was properly dressed before I went on parade, saw that I was dressed in time for dinner, valeted me, looked after my clothes and equipment, held himself responsible for my conduct, and indeed took complete charge of me. I believe the RSM would have had him on the mat if I happened to put a foot wrong. I rather liked having a valet. During my four years in the Army and, later on in life, my six years in India, I enjoyed that privilege. Even to this day, thirty-eight years later, when I have to clean my own shoes, or put studs in an evening shirt, or put away my clothes, I have a nostalgic yearning for the days when I had someone to do those sorts of things for me.

But to my task. At 7a.m. on that first morning, I found myself standing in front of a platoon of about seventy men. To say that I was a bit scared is to put it mildly. As a matter of fact I was scared stiff. That first parade, however, consisted of Company drill and doubling round the barrack square and, as I got warmed up, I lost my nervousness. I learned the words of command quickly enough and before very long I could handle my men with the confidence of an old hand.

My platoon looked a pretty tough lot. Most of them, as I learned later, were reservists and were accustomed to being called up annually for a month's training. Many of them were middle-aged and beery looking, the sort whose main interest in life was 'the price of a drink'. They were not easy to manage at first. They hated violent exercise. Physical jerks and doubling round the barrack square were anathema to them. The regular exercise and the ample food, however, soon began to tell and before very long they began to face their work cheerfully enough, and later to take a pride in their smartness.

I have in front of me now a group photograph of the officers, taken on 10 September 1914. There were fourteen Regulars and seven newly commissioned men who, like myself, had just joined after having had a month's training or so. We were lucky in having so many Regulars. Most of the Senior NCOs were also Regulars. We had not yet our full complement of junior officers but I think that by Christmas we had reached full strength. We were worked pretty hard in those early days. It was a case of physical jerks every morning from 7.00 to 8.00, parades 8.30 to 12.30 and 2.00 to 5.00, lectures in the evenings, route marches, sham battles, night operations, there was no respite. We newly appointed Temporary Officers, took our work very seriously. We were keen to win our spurs, as it were, keen to prove ourselves and to win the confidence of our seniors. And, by all accounts, we made marvellous progress. When we were not attending lectures, many of us spent our off hours in our rooms, where the Manual of Infantry Training and the Manual of Field Service became our constant companions. We rarely went over to the town. Indeed I can remember only one occasion when I did so.

There was one snag, one fly in the ointment. When I joined the battalion, the pay of a Second Lieutenant was 6s 8d a day and messing cost 10s a day minimum. To those of us who had no income, this placed us in a somewhat embarrassing position. It was not too long, however, until the position was rectified by raising our pay to 10s a day and cutting the messing to 7s 6d. In the case of the men, at that time a single man was paid 7s a week and a married man 3s 6d, the other 3s 6d being compulsorily retained and sent to his wife. In these circumstances there was little danger of any of us new recruits, officers or men, collecting a 'head like a concertina' or a 'tongue like a button stick'.

On 8 October we moved to the Royal Barracks, Dublin, and continued training on the same lines. We did a lot of our work in the Phoenix Park, which was quite close at hand. There we practised advancing to the attack in open formation and by short rushes, taking cover, patrol work, scouting, etc.

We also went for long route marches, twenty miles or so, and with both officers and men in full kit and carrying iron weights in our ammunition pouches. The latter we regarded as a great hardship and it is not surprising

Soldiers of the 6th Royal Irish Rifles, stationed at Fermoy, Co. Cork.

that the beastly iron weights often went missing. Though I never fell out on a route march, I was not all that good a marcher and I often suffered a good deal. My feet blistered easily and I tired more quickly than some of the others. The procedure on a route march was to halt and rest for ten minutes every hour. I used to say I could sleep for eight of those minutes.

Early in the New Year a batch of promotions came through. All the regular lieutenants were made captains, including our Company Commander, J.F. Martyr. Like many of the others, he had been waiting over ten years for his captaincy. He had also been engaged to be married for a number of years but could not afford to do so. Now he wasted no time; he got married as soon as he became a captain and stayed with his wife at the Royal Oak Hotel, near the Royal Barracks. One evening he invited me and the other officers of his company to meet his wife. I don't think I ever saw such a devoted and happy pair. But tragedy was close at hand, for he died of wounds after that fateful day on Gallipoli in August 1915, when the battalion went into action for the first time. We mourned the loss of a gallant officer and true friend. But what was our loss to that of his adoring wife who had waited so long for him?

Three other second lieutenants, Pollock, Brogden and McGavin, and myself were also promoted at that time. We were made Lieutenants. Another officer, G.B.J. Smith, who was gazetted on the same day as myself, 26 August, thought it most unfair that I should be regarded as senior to him and given my second pip before him just because of the fortuitous circumstance that my name began with a 'C' and his with an 'S'.

We fired a musketry course at Bull Island, Dollymount. The rifle range was at the north of the island. That was in the month of February and as far as I can remember the weather was fairly good. We used to march to the range, a distance of about ten miles. We were in good fettle by then and enjoyed the marches very much. The pavements rang as we swung along Ormond Quay and Bachelors Walk behind the band which usually accompanied us as far as O'Connell Street (then called Sackville Street). It was quite exhilarating.

We had to skirt the Royal Dublin Golf Links as we approached the Butts. I had begun to learn golf before the war broke out and the links attracted me. Then one day as we marched past, I saw a man drive off from a tee. It gave me the thrill of my life. Straight as a bullet the ball went. And what a length! I lost sight of it before it reached the end of its flight. To this day I can see that ball in the air.

On days when we marched to the Butts, we came back by tram, specially provided by the Dublin United Tramway Company (DUTC), 'specially', because we generally were a party of two or three hundred. In those days the trams were open topped.

While stationed in Dublin, I, and most of the junior officers, led a quiet life. Most evenings found us in our rooms studying our military manuals or attending lectures. I do not remember going into town or to a show of any kind on any one occasion, though I do remember going to a service in St Patrick's Cathedral a few times.

Early in February we marched to the Curragh in full kit. On the first day we went as far as Naas, a distance of nineteen miles. How well I remember that march. Every here and there the road had large patches of loose stones, and as the columns of four marched over them, crunch, crunch, crunch, you could hear the muttered oaths, swear, swear, swear. At Naas we billeted in the military barracks for the night. Pollock, McGavin and I were allotted a kitchen in the Warrant Officers' Quarters. It had a fire and a tiled floor. Wrapped in our great-coats, we huddled together on the floor, taking it in turn to wake up and tend the fire. It was a bitter cold night but, wearied as we were by the long march, we slept in spite of the cold and the hardness of the tiles. The chief trouble was to wake up in time to tend the fire before it went out.

The ten-mile march from Naas to our campsite at French Furze, near the western boundary of the Curragh, was even more trying than the nineteen-mile march of the previous day. As we left the shelter of the roadside hedges behind, after passing through Newbridge, with not a hedge or a tree in sight, we were met by a regular blizzard. A gale of wind blowing straight into our faces and drenching rain almost brought the column to a halt. The column was five or six hundred yards long and when a great gust hit it you could see the effect as the gust travelled along it, bending it till it almost looked like a long, wriggling snake. At times, parts were almost swept off the road. The waves reminded me of the waves set up in a meadow in the month of May when a breeze sweeps across it – a phenomenon I always loved to watch.

On arrival at the camp we found the whole place a sea of mud. There were lines of huts, each large enough to hold about fifty men. While they were under construction, the ground about them was cut up by the contractor's lorries and the ruts were now full of water. It was a dismal sight. The men sank to their ankles as they struggled to reach their allotted quarters. And when they reached them, as often as not, they found rain pouring through the roof.

The Officers' Quarters were more accessible as duck-boards had been laid along the huts. Each of us had a room to himself. Mine was not all that waterproof; it amused me to watch a floor rug that I had being lifted off the floor as the wind came rustling in through the cracks between the floorboards. In my broken-backed camp bed I found I needed as much clothing below me as above me if I was to keep warm.

When we had settled in and the roofs of the huts had stopped leaking and the ground had dried up and we had made paths here and there, the place assumed a pleasant enough appearance. Most of the Curragh is a wide open plain with no trees or hedges to break the force of the wind, but just behind our part of the camp there was an extensive area covered with clumps of furze bushes, hence the name 'French Furze', and in between the clumps, patches of grass, completely sheltered from the wind. It was my delight to select one of these for my afternoon's work, which generally consisted of lectures to my platoon, from the Handbook of Infantry Training. And if sometimes some of my class slept, I'm afraid that didn't worry me overmuch.

Life now began to be a bit more pleasant. We, the newly recruited officers, began to take more notice of each other. The feeling of tenseness engendered by the presence of our seniors was a thing of the past and we were able to relax, to feel at home. Now, too, we became more pally and began to form friendships. Nathan McGavin became my particular pal. He hailed from Glasgow, and I being of Scottish descent, we had something in common and took to each other from the start. During our stay at the Curragh he brought his sister Nan over on a visit and I brought the two of them to see my Uncle Charlie at Athy. He was a Scot of Scots and fell for the McGavins like several tons of bricks. I also took them to Knocknagee to meet my cousin Madge and her husband George. Later on, when Nathan and I were abroad, Nan paid Madge a visit a couple of times. Nan and I became friendly and kept up a correspondence till she took up an appointment as House Surgeon in a hospital in New York early in 1917, when we dropped it.

The first Guest Night I can remember was held when we had been about a month at the Curragh. I cannot recall who the guests were. Indeed all I can remember is the delightfully warm glow that coursed through my veins when, for the first time in my life, I had more than one glass of port at a single sitting. I don't think I had more than two on that occasion. I can also remember the warm feeling of comradeship that sprang up between myself and my two companions, Pollock and McGavin, that night, and I remember, too, how the duckboards swayed and heaved under my feet as I made my way towards my room when the time came for us to separate.

Life assumed a new aspect after these events. No longer did I feel alone or deserted. Instead I felt one of a band of very good companions.

In the month of February, the whole of our brigade, the 29th, assembled at the Curragh. It consisted of ourselves, the 6th Royal Irish Rifles, the 5th Connaught Rangers, the 6th Leinsters and the 10th Hampshires. Hitherto we had been doing company and battalion training, and had begun to feel a coherent body of men and to realise what a fine thing it was to be one of 800 men, swinging along the road or rushing into attack across the fields. Now, brigade field days, brigade route marches, brigade night operations, became the order of the day.

I got the fright of my life on one of these field days. I was detailed to bring my platoon to a point away on the north side of the Curragh. I don't know how it came about, but as I marched with my men along the road, I was stopped by a sentry who told me the butts of the rifle range were close to the road a little further along and that firing was

about to begin. I knew I could not possibly reach my ren-
dezvous if I had to retrace my steps and find another way,
so I forced the sentry to stand aside and let me through.
I knew it was a very wrong thing to do and that if I were
found out I should be for it. It was too awful to contemplate what would happen to me if one of us got hit by a
bullet coming over the butts; I should be court-martialled,
cashiered, jailed – dreadful! With my heart in my mouth I
hurried my platoon past the danger zone. For half a mile
we doubled as fast as we could go. We escaped, and the incident was never discovered, thank Heaven! but it haunted
my dreams for many a long day.

On 16 April as much of our division as was available
assembled on the Curragh and we had a 'March Past'.
The Divisional Commander, General Sir Brian Mahon,
GCVO, CB, DSO, took the salute. That parade made a wonderful impression on me. When the massed bands played
'God Save The King', and we presented arms, I became a
different man. A sense of loyalty suddenly sprang to life in
my breast and I became aware of a desire to serve my king,
to serve him to the uttermost. A couple of years later, when
I stood before him in Buckingham Palace and he shook my
hand, thanked me for my services and pinned the Military
Cross on my breast, I again thought of that moment on the
Curragh when I first pledged my loyalty to him.

We had no brass bands then, but the fife and drum
bands of the various units massed together and played
their regimental marches as the battalions and other units
marched past; slow time for the Rangers, medium time
for the Hampshires, quick time for the Rifles, all correct
and in order. It was a tiring day but being one of such a
stalwart body of men filled one with elation. We felt we
would be quite invincible.

Brigade training continued up to the end of April. It was
strenuous work, carried out in the bracing climate of the
Curragh, and by now we began to feel very fit indeed.

We were now moved across to England, to Basingstoke

in Hampshire where the whole of the 19th Division was assembled. The route chosen was via Larne and Stranraer. I have few recollections of the journey, but one thing I do remember. Shortly after we left Stranraer I poked my head out of the carriage window and cried, 'Hail, Scotland, land of my forefathers!' This was the one and only occasion on which I was in Scotland.

At Basingstoke our brigade was camped in tents in a field near the town. On one side of the field lay a huge wood which was also a game reserve. The story goes that the Munsters had pheasant for dinner the day after their arrival. They had some excellent poachers among them, apparently.

Divisional operations now took the place of brigade operations. Usually we left camp on a Tuesday, did a route march of fifteen or twenty miles or so and then bivouacked for the night in the shelter of a hedge or a bank if one was available. Reveille at dawn and breakfast cooked in the open, we then spent the day doing an attack or some other stunt, camping out again when the battle ended. On the third day we marched home again to our tents, having covered fifty or sixty miles in the three days. This sort of programme was carried on week after week. We were generally pretty tired when we got back, yet I remember that on one occasion Levis and I, on our return and having fed and had a bath, went for a stroll into Basingstoke, some two miles away; I admit I felt pretty sorry for myself on the way back.

The exercises were for the purpose of training the Divisional Staffs, but we poor footsloggers suffered all the hardships. Narrow, dusty, stony roads with high, overhanging hedges, on hot, suffocating days were things we shall never forget.

While at Basingstoke, the Division was inspected, first by the King and Queen and then by Lord Kitchener, who pronounced themselves highly satisfied with all they saw. I am sorry I missed both these occasions; I was away on special duty at the time.

We received some hospitality from the locals, and some of those who entertained us then afterwards visited me when I was in hospital at Highclere Castle. We were also able to obtain some local leave and on one occasion Pollock, McGavin and I visited Brighton where we dined in style at one of the posh hotels. Here I had a crème de menthe for the first time.

Thus, May and June went by pleasantly enough, and we almost began to think we'd never get away. Then, in the first week in July, our orders came through:

'Hold yourselves in readiness to serve in the Dardanelles!'

2

We Embark for the Dardanelles

July 1915

I have no recollection of all the fuss and bother of the preparations, or of the embarking, nor of our life aboard ship, till we reached Valetta. There the officers were allowed three hours shore leave and Pollock, McGavin and I went ashore and had a look around. The next stop was Alexandria and the next Mudros, where my Diary proper begins.

21 July 1915

On the morning of 21 July 1915, we awoke to find ourselves in the harbour of Mudros and we went up on deck to look around. The harbour, huge and almost completely closed, was crowded with shipping of all kinds; monitors, cruisers, a submarine or two, battleships, transport and troopships of various sizes. Some of the last of these we recognised. We had heard at Alexandria that they were missing, but all that had happened was that they had failed to call there; they had gone direct to Mudros and had beaten us in the race.

The shores of the harbour presented a rather repulsive prospect. There were no visible signs of vegetation. All was a dull, monotonous, sickly yellow. There was a camp, about fifty tents, on one side of the harbour, and on the other side there was a village which I failed to notice. I saw one peasant's cottage, a small, drab affair, hardly distinguishable from the hillside against which it stood.

At 0900 hours we began to disembark. We were taken ashore in small fishermen's boats, each of which held twenty men. Three of these boats at a time were taken in tow by a motor launch. The sea was a bit choppy and tossed the boats about but not dangerously. As a precaution we were ordered to loosen our belts and open our shoulder-straps. The boats were piloted by natives and I thought they were rather skilful in bringing the boats alongside the small timber jetty on which we landed. Some of us got a bit wet on the run ashore. The disembarkation went on apace and by 1400 hours the whole of the battalion and the stores had been safely landed. As we came ashore we squatted by platoons on the rough, stony, dusty ground.

A group of natives soon collected around us and sold tomatoes, about the size of plums, various kinds of melons and a kind of peppermint sweet. I smoked far too many cigarettes, ate tomatoes and lounged around.

As soon as all were ashore, we began to trail up to our bivouac area. No other word could describe the movement. The men were heavily laden, the ground was rough and hard and the dust, a thick yellow ochre, was absolutely suffocating. Four of my men carried my valise. They did not like the job. I helped with it myself most of the way.

The campsite was little more than a mile from the jetty at which we landed, but it took at least two hours to reach it. The last stage of the journey, a short stretch across open country, was the worst. It was at the level top of the hill we had just been climbing and it was littered with stones, each about the size of a turnip, with occasional boulders a couple of feet thick. The vegetation chiefly consisted of hard, prickly thistles, which bit through our putties. It was rough ground without a doubt and many a muttered oath escaped our dust-lined mouths as we struggled across it.

The ground allotted to us for our campsite was no better than we had just traversed. It was the most inhospitable I had ever met. However, we eventually got sorted and lined up by platoons and companies. Each man then set to work to clear a bed for himself and as soon as I had set my platoon to work, I began on my own bed. It was a tough job. I worked at it for about a couple of hours before I got it levelled and the stones removed. The surface of the ground consisted of baked clay as hard as rock and had to be hacked with an entrenching tool. Levis made his bed next to mine and Brogden and Harvey, the other platoon commanders, made theirs a couple of yards away. Captain Martyr, our Company Commander, had a stretcher so he had not much trouble with his. We had no tents or bivouacs. Our canopy was the dome of heaven and as we lay under it that first night, we were filled with amazement and wonder. Stars crowded the sky and winked and glowed and were brilliant. The Milky Way was a belt of stardust stretching from horizon to horizon, brilliant, beautiful.

There were other tasks to be done that first night before we could turn in. Blankets, provisions and water had to be carried up from the shore. Every one of us had to do the journey more than once. I was stupified with weariness before it was finished and have little recollection of the details, but I do remember turning in that night. l was quite content to accommodate myself to the conditions and was dozing off soon enough when Brogden woke me with a shout.

'Damn this noise', he cried, 'Damn those blithering crickets', and he pelted the ground around his bed with stones. He was more sensitive than I was and could never endure the noise they made. Several times during the night I heard him get up and beat the ground around his bed with a stick. It silenced them for a while, but very soon the infernal, monotonous din was resumed with more vigour than ever.

Our first consideration on waking next morning was regarding the construction of a sun shelter. We had no bivouac sheets or tents, as I have already mentioned, and we daren't use our groundsheets for this purpose; it would simply ruin them to expose them to the sun in this manner. We therefore decided to use our blankets. Someone discovered a pile of boards by a half-constructed jetty not too far away and we used them to support the blankets. They were rough structures and needed constant attention. We also made a dining shelter and a rough table and forms. It was well we had taken such prompt action for by noon orders were issued that none of these boards were to be touched. The shelters were somewhat inadequate and we had to wear our sun helmets when sitting under them.

The first couple of days we spent generally settling in, constructing cookhouses, making paths, clearing the area of stones, digging refuse pits, etc. The last of these was the hardest job of all. It involved digging into tough, sandstone rock. It took hours of work to make the smallest impression. As a consequence, our sanitary arrangements were hopelessly inadequate. The trenches for latrines and refuse pits were not anything like deep enough. Flies began to multiply immediately and sowed the seeds of dysentery which afterwards played havoc with the battalion.

Before very long a routine had been established and thereafter one day was very much like another. We paraded in the morning at 0500 hours for bathing and again at 1700 hours. During the day, except during the hottest hours, we did fatigue work. Water, rations and firewood had to be manhandled from East Pier, about two miles from the camp. We did very little training, a little musketry, platoon organisation and lectures, and on three occasions we practised night operations. Most of our energy was used up on fatigue work.

I associate many unpleasant things with our stay on this island of Mudros. The flies were a most infernal nuisance. They began to become numerous on the fourth day of our stay and thereafter they gave us no peace but punished us eternally. At mealtime they swarmed around us and their buzz was well-nigh intolerable. We kept our food covered as well as we could with cloths, handkerchiefs, etc. This was the manner of eating: you raised the corner of the cloth that covered your plate, secured a morsel of food on your fork or spoon and conveyed it to your mouth as fast as possible, at the same time lowering the cloth to its original position on the plate. If you were successful, you neither swallowed a fly nor allowed one under your plate cover. Partial failure was the general rule. Usually a fly or two succeeded in alighting on your mouthful before it reached your mouth and while you endeavoured to blow it off, you probably allowed several underneath your plate cover. Many a fly was swallowed, many an execration was uttered. Our mealtime conversation consisted of such as, 'Damn that fly!', or 'Damn those flies!', varied occasionally by 'Good Lord! I've swallowed another.' The only meal we enjoyed was dinner, which we postponed till after sundown. And not only during mealtimes did the flies pester us. A few generally managed to get inside our nets and make peaceful rest during the day rather difficult.

The flies had strong allies in the ants; small, black ones. They invaded our valises. They penetrated the food basket and got mixed up with the bread and raw meat. They were particularly partial to bully beef and simply wallowed in Nestlés condensed milk if they got the chance, and they often did. I hated the stuff myself, but Brogden and Levis could eat it in spoonfuls. Later on I learned to do the same.

I have already mentioned the crickets. I got used to them in time but I never got used to the thistles and the roughness of the ground. The heat too was a bit trying.

I now turn, and that with some avidity, to the redeem-
ing features of the place. First and chiefest there was
the bathing. We did enjoy it. The water was delightfully
warm and one could stay in for hours. A small wooden
pier was reserved for the use of the officers and it was a
truly lively scene from five till eight in the evening and
from five till seven in the morning. Everyone came. It was
more important than eating and ten times more enjoyable. Our General, Sir Brian Mahon, commanding the
10th Irish Division, often joined us, and thereby hangs a
tale. One evening he arrived as we were dressing. Here
was an opportunity of displaying his prowess that one of
our officers, Lieutenant Ryan, could not let pass. He was
half dressed; at least he had his shirt and his wristwatch on.
He saluted Sir Brian as he passed him, then, peeling off his
shirt, he greeted the General again with, 'A lovely evening,
Sir', and, taking a short race, he dived. It was a good dive
and he knew it, wherefore he wondered why everyone
laughed as he climbed on to the pier. Wondered, yes, until
he discovered he had forgotten to remove his wristwatch.
Wristwatches were scarce, too and there were no jewellers
in Mudros.

The men were somewhat pestered with what we called
sea urchins. They were something like hedgehogs and were
covered with black, sharp prickles. There was no bathing
pier for the men. They had to wade out to the deep water
and it was while doing so that their feet and knees came
in contact with these little black devils and received a rich
harvest of their thorns. These thorns were barbed and were
very hard to remove and if they were not removed quickly
they caused festering. As I was no swimmer, I, too, had to
wade into the deep water, over stones covered with sea-
weed and got my share of the prickles. It took me hours to
get them out.

There was a farmhouse near the bathing place and here
for the first time I saw the primitive, eastern method of
carrying out farming operations. They were exactly as

described in the Bible. The family were engaged in thresh-ing corn. Half a dozen oxen and ponies strung on a rope, which was attached to a central pole, marched round and round and trampled the grain from the ear. A young lad wielding a long whip saw that the animals kept their dress-ing and kept up the pace. When the treading was complete, the whole family turned out armed with forks and wooden shovels and tossed the stuff in the air until all the chaff and straw were blown away by the wind. Then they swept the grain into heaps and repeated the winnowing process until it was free from dust and chaff, when they stored it in bar-rels and bins.

Pack transport was the only form of transport they knew. Indeed it was the only form possible for there were no roads. Maybe they had no desire for roads, seeing as how they had no wheeled vehicles.

It was amusing to watch the peasants bringing home the harvest. You saw what at first you thought was a self-pro-pelled stack of sheaves with a boy walking in front of it, indeed often without the boy, and it was only when you approached it closely that you discovered there was an ass or a small pony inside it supplying the motive power. The loads those small animals were carrying appeared to be marvellous, and over such rough ground too. It looked cruel, but I don't suppose it was.

The ploughing was done with a pair of oxen, a yoke and a wooden plough. Of course, they only scratched the surface of the ground. The crops they produced were proportion-ally light, as one would expect.

One evening, I was sent on outpost with my platoon to a village about three miles from our camp. My duty would be to prevent anybody without a pass from entering the village. There were no roads, of course, so I marched to it across country, carefully noting landmarks so that I should not lose my way when coming back in the dark. Arriving at the village, I sent my platoon ser-geant round one way and, going in the opposite direction myself, I hoped we should discover the main entrances. There were, of course, no main entrances and there were dozens of minor ones. I discarded the idea of placing a sentry at each entry and, endeavouring to prevent anyone from entering the village, went through to the centre to see what had best be done. The village consisted of a large, disorderly, closely packed group of houses. There was one street a couple of hundred yards long in the centre. It did not by any means reach the outskirts but formed a cul-de-sac at both ends. Entry was gained to it through innumerable narrow alleyways. It was only in this street and around a square at the end of it that they were joined together. Elsewhere, each house stood in its own grounds, which extended no more than a couple of yards beyond its foundations. I found where the shops were and placed my men accordingly. We had exciting chases, caught one man and let the other two escape.

The peace and fresh coolness of this place was most attractive. It was in such contrast to the heat and glare and dust outside. The square made a charming picture. In the centre was a well with a pulley and bucket attachment. Around it stood a ring of olive trees with vines trailing from them. It was evening and the women came in groups, with jars or pitchers carried on their heads, to draw water. How good it tasted, cool and fresh and sweet, compared with the water we got in camp which was brought from Alexandria in barges and always tasted of petrol. The men came and sat in the rows of chairs placed outside the cafés and almost filled the square. They smoked and talked with many gesticulations and drank black, Turkish coffee. It was served in small cups with glasses of water. My men marched smartly to and fro or, when not on duty, sat under the olive trees. The village priest, tall and stately, with a long, black beard, sailed into the square, drank a cup of coffee and then moved from group to group with a word and gesture for each. The peace and simplicity of the scene impressed themselves indelibly on my mind,

and were it not for the presence of my men in uniform
and the occasional sharp sound of a military command,
I should have imagined that I had been transported to
Fairyland.

I left the village at 9.30 and reached camp at about 11p.m.
In the darkness, the ground felt a bit rougher than it did in the
daylight, nevertheless, we enjoyed the march home under the
light of the stars.

One thing I loved was to watch the lights in the harbour.
Their number was legion and I used to sit and watch them
for hours. I wondered what messages they winked to and
fro. Had our orders come through? Had the Bulgars come
in on our side? Then, too, they suggested civilisation; they
were a link with home. Perhaps the stars, too, were sending
messages. Perhaps they interpreted our thoughts, our vague
longings, and transmitted them to the hearts of those we
had left behind, at home.

I have but a few things more to mention before I get on
the move and leave the island behind for ever.

Our rations were none too good. I believe we got
fresh, or rather frozen, meat and bread once a week.
Otherwise they were bully beef and biscuit. Still, we did
not fare too badly. We were able to buy eggs, tomatoes,
melons, onions, lettuce and lemons and on one occasion
Brogden and Harvey procured a load of tinned salmon
in the village, and some tinned fruit. Besides, we had our
'chop box', which supplied us with cocoa, coffee, potted
meats, soup tablets, sauces, etc. Water was very scarce
and that used for drinking purposes was brought all the
way from Egypt. It was warm and not very fresh when
it reached us and was heavily chlorinated. It had to be
manhandled from the pier to the camp and as it was carried in petrol tins, it tasted of petrol. Water for cooking
was carried in dixies from wells sunk by the REs down
by the shore. It was not very clean and was brackish but
these qualities were submerged when it went into the
bully-beef stew.

Water, fuel and rations, as I have already mentioned, had to be manhandled from the pier to the camp, a distance of a couple of miles. Egyptian coolies were employed to do the unloading from the barges or ships which were used for transport. It was the first time I had seen coolies working and I was rather impressed by their prowess. No amount of work seemed to tire them. They were alike indifferent to the heat and the dust. As they toiled they sang, and it was always the same monotonous refrain, with clapping of hands and occasionally with what sounded like laughter. If their hands were engaged, their gaffers kept time for them. To me, it seemed weird, baffling, unfathomable. I thought of missionaries, but it seemed absurd. These men toiled with more patience and endurance than our men. What was their source of inspiration? Whence came their motive power? What made them so patient, so cheerful? Would you teach them higher things? Would you lift them out of the ruck and teach them more genteel ways? If you did, would they continue to do the dirty work? And if they refused, who would do it? These and many other equally unanswerable questions flitted across the field of my consciousness as I watched them. I was in touch with the East, the weird, fatalistic, unfathomable East, and who was I that I should unravel its mystery? I returned to my own work. I got on with the filling of the water carts.

On another day, from this pier, I made a trip to the *Aragon*, where GHQ had their headquarters. I was sent by our CO to draw cash for any officer who required it. I happened to be the first at the Field Cashier's Office and I received all I asked for, eighty-five pounds in gold. Those who followed me received a third of their demand. Mine had been promised me two days previously. The others did not know that. Ten months later, while crossing London, I met one of them. I did not know he had been there but it cropped up in our conversation. He told me how I had been sworn at that day. I am glad I did not know it at the time; the five sovereigns I had drawn for myself that day I brought with me to England.

Many a tale is told about the arrogance of the *Aragon*. It was aboard her, when I went out for the second time, that I learned them from the stewards, so they must have had some foundation. When she left Mudros, she could do only four knots, so heavy was the load of barnacles on her bottom. When first they tried to move her they found she was aground on champagne bottles!

Visitors were given a frosty reception. Whether on business or otherwise, they were met with a 'what the devil are you doing here?' kind of look, 'there's a boat that will take you ashore ... Lunch here? this is not a floating hotel ... There's an ASC depot ashore, they'll give you your rations.' Such were the expressions the non-red-tabbed were met with. Lord Kitchener put an end to all that sort of thing when he came East.

A few days before we left Mudros, the Home Mail was brought in, the first since we had arrived. That, indeed, was a day to be remembered. Eagerly we watched while the letters were sorted. It was McGavin did the sorting. He sat at a table in battalion HQ Mess and the rest of the officers formed a circle round him. How pleased I was when he called my name! The others, no doubt felt the same when theirs were called. And poor McGavin, there was none for him and he was the first to run for the mailbag. There were seven for me, twelve for Brogden, two for Levis, etc. How we gloated over them, bragged about them, announced how many we got! How important they seemed that day! If the writers only knew the pleasure they gavel; but maybe they did. Some were from mutual acquaintances and were passed round. They were from the friends we had made in Dublin, the Curragh, Basingstoke. Others were private and we retired to our bivouacs to enjoy them. The rest of the day we spent answering them and most of the next too. Perhaps we felt that once we went into battle opportunities for letter writing would be few and far between.

It was wonderful how the arrival of the letters cheered up our spirits. Everyone had a cheery greeting for everyone else,

'Hello! Lovely evening!'

'Topping!'

'News from home?'

'Yes', and smile answered smile and the heat and the dust were forgotten.

Signs that the day of our departure was approaching now began to multiply. Maps were issued, not of Gallipoli but of the mainland. It was rumoured that it was there we should land and that we should work our way up the south side of the straits. Pamphlets were issued describing the conditions there and we lectured our men on them. We discussed the possibilities amongst ourselves, tentatively, in fits and starts that showed how continuously our minds dwelt on the subject. We began to get superstitious. No one would any longer dream of 'making a third', or of not throwing salt over his left shoulder if he happened to spill any.

Kit inspections now became the order of the day. Some couldn't keep a complete kit for more than a day. They'd break your heart. There was some stealing and this was treated as the most heinous of crimes. One culprit was given six hours Field Punishment No. 1; he was tied to the wheel of a water cart, feet off the ground, arms and legs extended. His yells disturbed the three adjacent camps and struck terror into our hearts. He sobbed, he wept like a child, he begged for mercy, but it was of no use, he was made to suffer the full penalty. It put a stop to a good deal of the 'stealing from a comrade on active service'.

Now we were issued with three days' iron rations. These had to be carefully watched.

We spent three Sundays on the island but had only one Church Parade. It was a most impressive one. We formed a hollow square round a huge boulder that stood on the side of the sun-baked hill and looked like an altar, and the chaplain, the Revd Crozier, looked like an ancient prophet.

He spoke brave and manly words that reached our inner-most hearts. It was the eve of our going into battle, our first battle, and he rose to the occasion nobly. I do not remember what he said, but I do remember that I went away from the simple service full of courage and high hopes and confidence.

On the second of August it was announced that each Company should choose a subaltern and thirty men to be left behind as a first reinforcement. This was an exciting moment. Would it be a disgrace to be chosen? We thought it would. We discussed every possibility as if our lives depended on it (as indeed they did), as if more than our lives, the Colonel's opinion of us, depended on it. What considerations would he take into account? Efficiency? Inefficiency? Seniority? Juniority? What a sigh of relief I gave when I found my name was not amongst those selected! If it had been, I felt sure I would have died of a broken heart.

I often wondered if they were ever sent to Gallipoli. There was certainly a need for them to fill up the gaps left in our ranks after the first few days' fighting, as it proved. On the evening of 3 August they bade us good-bye and moved into a new camp. I wondered what their feelings were.

On the evening of the fourth, word was brought to us, as we were having our usual dip, to return to camp immediately. I walked back with Levis. Of course we guessed what was up; we felt the hour had struck. When we reached camp we learned that preliminary orders had already been issued and found that preparations for the departure were in full swing. There was an undercurrent of excitement. I can't say that we rejoiced at the prospect of being in touch with the real thing at last, but there was excitement. At the very least it was a change from the monotonous routine of the preceding days.

I had not much to worry about; just my platoon and myself. The men had a difficult job to get all their stuff into their packs. The three days' rations which were issued, and which they had to carry, added to their difficulty. I took my valise and Brogden took his, but the majority of the officers left theirs behind them. I never used mine on Gallipoli, nor did the others, except three. We were not there long enough.

3

Gallipoli

5 August 1915

Reveille sounded at 4a.m. and we had breakfast, packed up
and were on the move at 7a.m., our orders being to be on
the beach by eight o'clock.

We thought we should embark immediately, but no
such luck. It was 3p.m. before we began and it was six
o'clock before the last man was aboard. All through the
day we lay on that hard, stony, dusty beach, nibbled at
our rations and smoked – smoked far too much. We were
able to buy chocolate, tomatoes and peppermint from
the villagers. These helped to keep us from being too
bored. At noon we decided to have a regular lunch, so
we bought a helmet-full of tomatoes, a few melons and
opened a couple of tins of bully beef. We also acquired a
'chatty'. It held our drinking water and kept it delightfully cool. It was here I had a lesson in putting up with
things. The Colonel happened to come up while we were
feeding and Captain Martyr asked him if he would care
to join us.

'Thank you', he said,' I shall be delighted', and held out
his hand for a helping of 'bully'. And he received it on his
hand, straight from the tin from which our worthy captain
extracted it with a jackknife. He had a couple of tomatoes

Gallipoli.

with it and a ration biscuit. Then he wiped his hands in the dust and had a swig of water from the chatty from which all of us had been drinking. We had used our canteen lids as plates and our knives and forks from the chop box. He was independent of them and appeared to enjoy his meal more than we did.

It was a relief when the order was given to embark. Our transport, *The Partridge*, was a small passenger ship that used to ply between Belfast and Larne and made occasional voyages to the Isle of Man and perhaps, once in a while, ventured as far as Liverpool. Who would have thought, before this tremendous cataclysm which threatened to overwhelm the world had broken upon us, that she would ever tread the waters of the Aegean?

We were well over a thousand strong, brigade HQ being with us, so only the officers had room to sit down. The men were crowded all over the ship and it was impossible to keep the Companies separate.

Towards evening, other transports, which had been loaded overnight, began to move off. Three passed close to us. We gave them a ringing cheer and they answered with a jubilant shout, then disappeared in the gathering dusk, a grim, silent procession, but nevertheless pathetic, heart-searching. I could not but wonder how many of them would never return to their homes, their kindred, their loved ones. It is in moments like these that we realise the awfulness, the sadness, the deep pathos of war. Its terror, its frightfulness, its glory are not thought of, only its sadness. Soon we followed them into the night.

A dark, spectral shadow appeared on our right. Somebody was heard to say, 'That's Gallipoli.' We gazed at it in silence through the gloom. 'There they go'; we heard a dull booming in the distance. It was the guns. Whose? We did not know. We drew nearer. I went round to the other side of the ship.

'Ha! Did you see that flash?'

'There's another and another.'

The sounds were now quite distinct. Louder and louder they grew, and sharper. We could see the flames leap from the guns' mouths; we could see the scattering of fire as the shells burst. Brilliant searchlights illuminated the hillsides. A stream of whitest light mounted the heavens and burst into a sheet of flame. Thereafter a thousand ribbons of light, red and green and white, curved towards the earth. It was a Turkish star shell. Absorbed and yet fearful we watched.

Somebody said, 'Our monitors are bombarding the Turkish positions'. The words sounded like a distant echo. Almost unnoticed, they floated across the field of my consciousness, but they eased the tension.

Suddenly there was a crash on our starboard quarter. There was a burst of flame and in the midst of it a pillar of water. A searchlight swung round towards us. Were we spotted? Were we being shelled? I felt a tightening in the muscles of my chest. I'm sure I turned pale. The light swung away again and settled on a jut of land (Gaba Tepe). I heard someone say, 'There's a Turkish post there. Our guns are shelling it.' My heart beat again. Our time was not yet.

We were now about two miles from the shore. We heard the rattle of rifle and machine-gun fire, faintly at first, then more and more clearly. It began on our right, then spread in a semicircle round to our left. It grew in volume and intensity until the whole semicircle rattled and sputtered. Star shells and Very lights became ten times more numerous. The enemy guns woke to life and filled the air close to us with bursts of flame. Surely there was an attack on. God pity those in the midst of that inferno!

We drew nearer. Anzac Cove, for which we were making, became discernible. The land appeared to rise steeply from the shore, almost perpendicularly, and it was dotted over with lights. It looked like a village, but of course it was a village of dugouts, sheltered from the enemy by the steepness of the hill behind it.

When we were about half a mile from the beach, our nostrils were assailed by a peculiar smell. Pollock was standing beside me. He noticed it too. Then it dawned on us. It was the smell of decaying animal matter, of dead men's flesh and bones; the flesh and bones of the Australians and New Zealanders who had fallen there in their first attack on Anzac. We shivered at the gruesome idea.

At about eleven o'clock we drew alongside, or rather barges came alongside us, and we began to disembark. All was now hurry and bustle. Forgotten the vague speculations it gave rise to in our minds. The spell was broken and we lost ourselves in action.

The Companies had been somewhat mixed up on board and owing to the crush it was impossible to sort them out then, so we just filed ashore as we came to the gangway. Captain Martyr and Brogden and I kept together, but I do not know where Levis and Harvey, the other two officers of 'A' Company, had got to. They evidently boarded the next lighter. From the lighter, by means of planks, we scrambled on to the jetty. It was of timber and the end had been shattered by shellfire.

It was equally impossible to sort the men out on the foreshore; it was so narrow and steep. Besides, it was quite dark and so the order was given to move off as we landed. Guides were provided and we filed off into the darkness. It was difficult going. The path was steep and narrow and our feet sank in the thick, sandy dust that covered it. We moved in single file; we were heavily laden and so it was hard to keep in touch. We were going for I don't know how long, two or three hours perhaps. There were many checks and sometimes we had to step out so as not to lose touch. I helped Brogden to carry his valise.

At length we halted and were ordered to fall out. The moon had risen by now and we could see what we were doing. The men were not all in yet but they came along by degrees and joined their respective Companies. We found a comparatively flat place and lay down for a breather. Brogden took off his boots and got into his valise. Levis and I lay down together to keep warm (he and Harvey had caught up after we disembarked). I may have slept but I am not certain. Anyhow it seemed that almost immediately we lay down, the order came through to 'fall in'. Brogden said 'Damn!' as he hastened to put on his boots. We shouldered our packs and moved further up into the gully, and here we halted for the rest of the night. The sides of the gully were so steep that it was impossible to find a flat place where one could make a bed. Leaving my pack aside, I went to collect those of the men who had not yet come in. I got a few of them in, but I might as well have saved myself the trouble; most of them had taken their packs off and found a reasonably flat place where they could lie down and I couldn't get them to budge. It was near morning anyhow and we were dog-tired after spending the night on our feet, so I did not insist. About an hour before dawn I returned to Company HQ and lay down on the least steep part of the slope I could find.

The sound of the fighting just above us on the brow of the hill again reached my consciousness. It was not so fierce as when we were landing. There was a steady patter of rifle fire and occasional bursts of machine-gun fire. Curious how it ran up and down the line, died away and then burst out again. Shells shrieked to and fro across our heads, but none of them came near us.

I was soon asleep, but it was not for long for as soon as dawn broke we had to be up and doing. Our first job was to collect our Platoons, which were still a bit mixed up, and this done, we immediately began digging in. Every man had a pick or shovel which he had brought with him from Lemnos. We first of all made tiers in the slope and then undermined the upper sides so that by lying closely in we could obtain some shelter from shells coming across the hill. It was every man for himself and as hard as he could go. Levis and I dug in together. Capt. Martyr, Brogden and Harvey dug in a couple of yards away. Egad, it was tough work, as tough as it was on Lemnos. Every ounce required a separate stroke of the pickaxe.

Our dugout was much better than the one the other officers made. We had worked harder, more continuously and longer. The other was untenable during certain periods that morning. Ours was fairly safe, even in the hottest periods. We kept a small fire going while we were digging and dealt out frequent supplies of cocoa until our supply of water ran out. I don't know how we would have stuck the unaccustomed work if it hadn't been for it. The toil told on our hands; mine were frightfully blistered.

At eleven o'clock it began – the shelling, I mean.

It was our first time under shellfire and we wondered how we would take it, and indeed I do not know what effect it would have had on me were it not for the example set out before us. On the opposite side of the gully, Shrapnel Gully it was called, were a couple of companies of Australians. They had been shelled several times during the morning but they continued about their duties as if nothing were happening. So, when it came to our turn, we tried to emulate them. We pretended we were just as indifferent as they appeared to be. It did not quite come off, though. There were not many heads to be seen during the first half hour. The first man that was hit kicked up a terrible racket. It took four men to bring him in. He was not very badly hurt but his nerve was completely shattered and every time a shell burst near at hand, or guns went off, he tried to break away. He shouted and sobbed aloud and quite put the wind up those who heard him. Maybe many of us would have done the same thing had it happened to us. We were holding ourselves tense, our nerves tightly strung and if, as in the case of the one mentioned, we had been the victim, we should probably have given a similar display.

After a while we began to get used to it and the 'shocks' diminished in force, and seeing that so little damage was being done, we began to move about more freely. We learned where the bad spots were and took care to avoid them.

Still, we had some bad times that day; even the Australians were glad to scuttle into their burrows. 'B' Company had a large part of its rifles and equipment burnt or buried and had to move to a fresh site. They crowded on the path in front of our area. Battalion HQ also had to move. Some of our dugouts were blown in too and a lot of our equipment destroyed. No water could be drawn till after sundown, the vicinity of the wells being under fire. The QM Stores were also in an unhealthy spot.

I slept for a couple of hours in the afternoon. When I woke up my legs were covered in rubble which had rolled in from the slope above my dugout. There were bits of shrapnel amongst the rubble. The dugout on my right where the orderlies had been lying had disappeared and Capt. Martyr's dugout had been damaged. There was nobody near me. Shells were falling fairly close. It must have been pretty hot around me while I slept.

Later on that day we were issued with small squares of white cotton and instructed to sew them on our jackets, one on each sleeve and one on the back. We were evidently going into a night attack and they were for the purpose of enabling us to distinguish friend from foe. Levis and I sat side by side in our dugout while we sewed them on. One of the orderlies, whose dugout had been damaged, crept in behind us. He was shivering with fright and every time a shell burst nearby we felt him shrinking more closely to the back wall. It left very little room for us in the dugout and whenever we raised our heads they hit against the roof and knocked clay and sand down our necks. Our position was uncomfortable, to say the least of it, but we kept on sewing and it kept our minds off the other things.

It was nearly dark when at last we got permission to draw water. Brogden and Harvey took charge of the operation. Rations were drawn but not distributed and orders were issued that we should be ready to move off at 11p.m. We packed our valises and the men their packs. I got my men together as best I could and, having seen that they had sewn on their white patches, I got them to lie down for a rest.

There was a good deal of noise over the top of the hill just above us at that time. The machine guns were hard at it and there was incessant rifle fire. The gunners too were working hard and the boom rang up and down the gully. The men were a bit rattled. Indeed, so were all of us. We had little to say to one another just then. About this time, it was just getting dark, I went into my dugout. There was somebody lying across the back of it, I think it must have been Levis, and I lay down and used his chest as a pillow. I fell asleep immediately. When I awoke, he was gone and indeed for a moment I thought everyone was gone and I was left behind. It was not quite as bad as that, however. I found the Company had fallen in. My men were huddled together on the path. Only half of them had their equipment and rifles. I got hold of my two sergeants but could not get them to do anything. They were properly dazed. One of my corporals, however, proved to be a tower of strength and between us we managed to collect the packs. Then we began to search for rifles and other equipment, picks, shovels, etc. It was pitch dark overhead, but the whole gully was lighted up continually with a rain of bursting shells and star shells. This was the worst time we had had so far. I thought I would never get my men kitted out and I was feverishly excited. The din was awful. Several times I thought I had everything but when I inspected my platoon there was someone still short of a rifle or set of equipment. It was heartbreaking. In the end, however, we succeeded and when we marched off, the only one short of a rifle was my Platoon Sergeant.

Then there were rations to be issued. One of my sergeants had, by this time, somewhat recovered and other NCOs were able to help. The bacon was cut into chunks and distributed. The men were persuaded to pack a lot of jam into their haversacks, already full. We crammed fistfuls of sugar and tea into their pockets, also biscuits.

While we were thus busily engaged, the din of the battle almost escaped our notice but now, as we waited for the command to move, it returned with full force. The shelling seemed to be traversing towards us and to have reached a point only a hundred yards or so further up the gully. Thank God we moved off before it came too near. Once we got on the move we began to feel better. Movement eased the tension in out chests and we breathed more freely. Ribald remarks were to be heard and, now that we were moving away from what appeared to be a veritable hell, we jested about it. I heard even a laugh or two. It was a terrific relief.

We were on the move for the greater part of that night. Twice, or it maybe three times, we turned and retraced our steps, and the usual remarks could be heard about the blind leading the blind. In these interminable gullies, map reading must have been almost impossible, especially at night. We juniors had no idea where we were. We were glad when we were given the order to halt and fall out for a couple of hours. We did not take off our equipment and I warned my men to keep a tight hold of their rifles. I lay down on my back across the road in front of my Platoon, using my gas helmet as a pillow, and gazed up at the stars. It was almost as bright as day. I was soon asleep and did not move until wakened by the chill morning air.

7 August 1915

We were in Dead Man's Gully and, from the gruesome smells that clung to the morning air, one could not but conclude that the name was well deserved. To the north, south and east, the sides of the gully showed up steep and rocky. The ground was parched and devoid of vegetation. To the west, the gully wound down to Anzac Cove.

Here it looked as if we should be well sheltered from hostile snipers, but as soon as dawn broke, we were ordered to get our men under cover as we should probably remain here for some hours. Cover was not difficult to find as the sides of the hill were terraced and contained numerous dugouts. We took advantage of these and were soon comfortable enough. From a pile of cases of bully beef on the other side of the gully we obtained sufficient wood to make fires on which to cook our breakfasts, which were necessarily simple as each man had to cook his own, using his canteen to make tea, taking the water from his bottle. There was no central cooking on this occasion.

As we were under orders to be ready to move at a moment's notice, we did not dare go very far from where we lay, but during the morning Brogden and Harvey managed to return to Shrapnel Gully and procure some provisions from the chop box. They were very welcome, especially the tinned fruit, for our thirsts were unquenchable.

During the day, Levis and I went for a short stroll up the hillside, choosing a path that led up and over the closed end of the gully. Before reaching the crest, the path cut straight through the hill forming a kind of huge gateway. Going through this, we found that the ground fell away on all sides and suddenly revealed to us with startling effect a most wonderful view. A great, semicircular horn ended in a huge spire, a deep cleft separating it from the hillside and wedged in this cleft we could distinctly see the form of a soldier, apparently standing upright. It was the dead body of a British sniper. How he reached that point we could not imagine, and it was evidently too difficult a task to remove the body or they would hardly have left it there. To us, unused as we were to the horrors of war, it was a gruesome spectacle.

Looking at our maps, we could make out the wide, beautiful sweep of the shore of Suvla Bay. Inland, Salt Lake glittered dazzlingly white. Lala Baba raised itself in the middle distance and threw back the waves of the Aegean. These received but a glance. Further inland was a more compelling, thrilling sight. The whole low range of hills surrounding the Salt Lake were enveloped in clouds of white smoke through which darted bursts of red flame. This was especially concentrated around the village of Anafarta, two or three miles from where we stood. The village was obviously on fire and dense clouds of smoke rolled away from it towards the south. Turning our eyes to the left, we saw from whence came the shells. There, in the bay, lay our monitors, tongues of flame every now and then darting from their sides. After a time we made out the infantry, barely distinguished spots of khaki, advancing in waves from the beach. The patter of musketry and the rattle of machine-gun fire supplied a treble, on our right, to the deep bass of the guns of the monitors on our left. The whole pageant of battle was verily and indeed spread before our eyes. Unknown to us at the time, we were witnessing the Suvla Bay Landing, soon to become famous. And who will condemn us if we gazed in awe at the splendid scene ourselves? Pondering these thoughts in our hearts we returned to our dugout.

A strong wind had sprung up and chased like fury through the narrow gullies, whirling with it sandy dust that lay everywhere around. We were glad to seek shelter from it and we set about preparing our evening meal. Through the rest of this day and the following night we remained in this gully, always waiting for the word to move.

8 August 1915

The order to march reached us on the morning of the 8th and we moved off through the gap Levis and I had already explored and proceeded down towards the beach. Here we entered a communications trench where we met endless streams of pack mules loaded with ammunition and rations, and columns of troops moving in the opposite direction. At last we emerged and were drawn up under a knoll close to the beach. Here we remained for three or four hours, under the full blast of the midday sun. Some of the men, who straggled somewhat towards the end, were spotted by Turkish snipers who opened fire on them and sent them scampering to the shelter of the knoll. Two or three were wounded.

During the afternoon we received our orders. They were, 'Make good Hill "Q" at dawn. Farm "B" is already in our hands!' That was all. Now that I have been through a few properly organised attacks, I realise how totally inadequate they were. We could see Hill 'Q' on the distant horizon, Chanuk Bair it was, the highest point on the Sari Bair Ridge, the highest on the peninsula, for that matter, and, as we afterwards discovered, the centre of the main attack, the crux of the whole position.

About three o'clock in the afternoon we began to move. In order to reach a dried-up riverbed which would

lead us towards our objective, we had to cross a saddle of
exposed ground, a projection of the knoll behind which
we were drawn up. This was under the observation of the
Turkish gunners and, as soon as the head of our column
appeared on it, they opened fire. We were then ordered to
rush across the exposed stretch by platoons. Harvey, with
No.1 Platoon, led the way. I followed with No.2, marching
in file. The shells whistled low over our heads and burst
harmlessly fifty or a hundred yards beyond us. Brogden followed with No.3 at the double and had a few close shaves.
Thereafter the platoons doubled across as best they could.
The Turks had now the range and hammered away for all
they were worth. 'D' Company had a rough time. One of
its platoons was so badly mauled that it did not follow the
rest of the battalion into action. Their CSM and several
sergeants were killed. This news trickled up to us at the
head of the column as we pushed our way up the dried-up
watercourse. We tried to keep from ducking. We realised
that now, at last, we were honoured by the personal attention of the enemy.

It was about this time that I had the first casualty in
my platoon. It occurred during a hold-up. The head
of the column had taken a wrong track with the result
that we had to turn back until it could extricate itself.
In the meantime the rear platoons had pushed forward
and there was no room for the head of the column to
get back and on to the right track. At this moment, the
Adjutant, Captain Eastwood, killed next day, came along
and ordered those nearest it to get on to a piece of level
ground on the right of, and above, the level of the track.
They obeyed promptly, but one man, McCann by name,
hesitated. I ordered him to get up at once and helped him
to climb the low bank by pushing him from behind. No
sooner had he mounted the bank than he received a bullet
in the temple and rolled back as if he were dead. He was
not killed; the bullet had grazed his skull along his temple
but had not penetrated.

We applied a dressing as quickly as possible and laid him on the ground. There he lay, quivering from head to foot. I was sure he was dying and thought every quiver would be his last. Naturally enough, he blamed me for forcing him into an exposed position. With the finger of accusation pointed at me, he cried out, 'I'm dying, I'm dying. It was him, it was your fault. Oh, I'm dying', and all the time, he shook and quivered as if verily and in truth he was about to breathe his last. We placed him on a stretcher and sent him back. And he did not die after all but in due course arrived safely home in Blighty. This incident was somewhat upsetting, but after a little while we recovered and took advantage of the temporary halt to make ourselves a spot of tea in our canteens.

At about six o'clock we were led aside into a cup-like hollow and told we should be here for a couple of hours. The CO then informed us that Achi Baba had fallen, but somehow the news did not elate us. Perhaps it was that we were too dazed to take it in, which may have been just as well for it proved to be untrue. Achi Baba was our main objective.

It was while here that I first came into contact with the Turks. I was instructed to post a picket on the rim of the hollow in which we were halted and when I got there I found Turks in plenty – dead ones. I stumbled across them, I trod on them, I picked my way amongst them. They were all over the place. I found a trench nearby and this I selected as a suitable place for a picket. Dead bodies lay round about and it was not at all a salubrious spot. The men did not like it and besought me not to leave them there too long. I promised to relieve them at midnight and they seemed satisfied and began to settle down.

While reconnoitring this position I happened to show myself on the skyline. The second time I did so I was greeted by a volley of rifle fire. Half a dozen bullets phutted into the parapet of the trench. A third time I was greeted in a similar manner. They came fairly close, too, for they kicked sand and gravel into my face. I decided it was better not to expose myself just there.

On returning to Company HQ, I found the others settling down for the night. A Bosche aircraft circled overhead for a few minutes and then flew off again. Brogden and I set to clear a place where we could lie down. It was difficult as the ground was covered with roots and stumps where it was not overgrown with gorse. We spent an hour working at it, then, as luck would have it, just as we lay down, word came that we were to fall in.

How shall I describe the night that followed? It was the most wearying, the most trying, the most nerve-racking I have ever been through. We set out about an hour after dusk; we were still on the move at dawn. All night we blundered forward, now halting, now moving at a snail's pace, now struggling forward as fast as we might over the uneven ground. As the night wore on the halts became more and more distressing. The men slept in their tracks. To rouse them to keep the column from breaking was indeed a most difficult and heartbreaking task. More than once, I myself dozed off for a few moments. Once I awoke to find the column moving past me. I rushed forward, fear gripping at my heart, and was relieved to find I was only a few paces from the head of my platoon. And if, during a halt, some two or three men failed to wake up in time when the advance was resumed, what would happen then? The rest of the Company would sleep on, unaware that they were being left behind. A dreadful contingency to contemplate. A hundred times I went back to the head of the next platoon to make sure it was in touch, that there was no gap. To add to the difficulty of keeping in touch, there was a continuous stream of wounded passing down, and ammunition mules were constantly passing to and fro. A break did occur eventually, and in my platoon, too. It was at a very awkward place in the track. The ground suddenly rose steeply, culminating in a cleft-like gap and a ledge. You required to use both hands to get through it. Then the ground fell away in a gradual slope. When I got through the gap, I could see the next man in front of me forging ahead as fast as he could. I hurried after him, just keeping him in sight. This fast pace lasted for about twenty minutes. Then there was a halt and then I discovered that half my platoon was missing, and with it the rest of the Company. I reported the matter and some-body swore at me.

I started back up the hill in search of the rest of the column. It was just getting light and I could see paths leading hither and thither to left and to right. How I dreaded that I shouldn't remember my way back, or that the column would have moved on before I had rejoined it. At one moment I hesitated as to whether or not I should turn back. Again I doubled up the hill. At last I found them. The next thing I remember is that we had joined up with the head of the column and were halted in a deep gully, all serene.

A steep, dark hill (Rhododendron Ridge) loomed up in front of us, sprinkled here and there with small lights. Intermittent rifle fire sounded all around us and gradu-ally increased in volume as the light improved. We were obviously approaching the front line. It was better that no lights should be shown. I warned my men accordingly and gave orders that no smoking would be allowed. Dawn now broke and the weary night march came to an end.

9 August 1915

We were collected in a deep gully and the officers, sitting down on the ground, discussed the situation. In front of us was the hill which we knew was our objective. Just then, McGavin rushed up, breathing hard with excitement and announced, '"B" and "D" Companies are missing. The Hampshires have lost touch with us.'

The CO and the Adjutant hurried past, orderlies ran hither and thither, excitement reigned everywhere.

I overheard the CO and our Company Commander, Captain Martyr, discussing the possibility of attacking with two companies instead of two battalions (our battalion was to have been in support of the Hampshires in the attack). The dilemma seemed to exercise the attention of our senior officers for perhaps half an hour. Then, with a sigh of relief, we learned that contact had been re-established and we resumed our advance.

The sun had now risen and we could see what lay around. The place was frightfully wild. On all sides rose steep, almost inaccessible hills covered with a dense growth of holly, laurel and fig. What a country to fight over! It looked impossible. The track we followed was a dry watercourse. In places the banks were high, rocky, overhanging. Huge boulders lay here and there, and amongst the boulders were the bodies of those who had fallen as they fought their way up on the previous days. Bodies of the defenders were there too; the latter seemed to be more numerous. When, later in the day, I came back wounded, I thought there were a good many more bodies there. Meanwhile, our monitors were bombarding the crest of the hill. Later these were joined by the guns of the battleship *Queen Elizabeth*. To us, who had never previously witnessed a bombardment, the sight was most impressive. We thought the whole side of the hill was being lashed and torn. Huge masses of earth were being heaved into the air and dense columns of smoke appeared, followed by a ripping and crashing as of thunder. To us it was a noble and inspiring sight.

We were now climbing the lower slopes of a hill through a dense growth of evergreens. 'A' and 'B' Companies were to lead the assault, supported by 'C' and 'D' Companies. Advancing thus, we reached a bank some three feet high, which marked the edge of the scrub. Beyond it lay a fairly level field of corn, almost white in colour and less than a foot high.

I crouched behind this with my platoon. Owing to the steepness of the slope and the dense undergrowth, however, it was impossible to collect them all together. Then came the order, 'Assault enemy trenches! Numbers one and three platoons leading, numbers two and four in support!'

About fifty yards to my left, I saw Lt Brogden mounting the parapet. 'Come along, Campbell!' he shouted, and waving my hand in reply I gave the order to my men and rushed forward, followed by the nearest of them. My rush brought me about fifty yards, then I threw myself on the ground and looked around to see how many men had followed me. I thought about half my platoon had done so. Just then, before I had time to do anything more, I received a bullet through the calf of my leg. During our next rush, I realised that the band of my puttee had been cut and was getting entangled around my legs. When we were on the ground again, I made some attempt to tie it up, but my fingers were nervous and clutching and covered in blood. I got it tied somehow, however, and seeing some cover in the form of low scrub ahead, I dashed for this and did not stop until I reached it. Few of my men followed me thus far. I did not know how many of them had become casualties, and I did not dare to go back and see. All this time we were under heavy rifle fire from the Turkish trenches. My hands and face were pitted and scratched with the stones and earth kicked up by the bullets. How I escaped being hit again I do not know.

The place I had reached afforded a certain amount of cover and many of the troops who had preceded us during the previous attack had taken advantage of it. We had not been told that any of our own troops were ahead of us. However, I threw myself on the ground amongst them. One of them immediately offered me his water bottle; he had spotted that I was wounded. I took a swig from his bottle, though my own was not quite empty, and felt much revived. The same lad then set to and helped me to dress my wounded calf, using his own 'First Aid Field Dressing'. While thus engaged, he was hit in the foot. I helped him to remove his boot and to apply a dressing to his wound, using my kit. This done, I had time to look around and see what was happening.

I found I had crossed a wheat field; bearded wheat, it was, overripe and about six inches high. To my right the field of wheat swung forward and became much wider; to my left, where Brogden had crossed, the patch of scrub bent backwards towards the bank from which we had jumped off. All along the edge of the scrub was a line of wounded and dead. The cover was deceitful and time and again I saw a wounded man being hit again. One man, a few yards away from me, rolled and twisted in agony. I yelled to him to keep quiet and get under cover, but just then there was another 'phutt', and with a sickening 'wumph', he rolled over and remained still.

Away to the right, a Company of the Hampshires were pelted with shrapnel as they tried to dig in. Another Company was working its way forward under cover of a hedge of hazels.

When I had been halfway across the wheat field, I had seen Lieutenant Smith dashing forward at the head of his platoon. During his first rush, I heard him give a mighty yell. I saw him fall to the ground where he rolled over and over, clutching at his puttee.

I saw no troops succeed in getting across the field. In front of me and about a hundred yards distant was a ragged line of infantry lying on their faces on the ground. They were not digging in, nor were they firing, they were just lying still. Behind them, scattered over the ground were many others, also ominously still. These, I learned afterwards, had advanced to their present position just before the day dawned, and there, with the advancing day, they were wiped out, almost to a man. Those whom I had overtaken were the supports, who had not been able to reach their front line.

Just beyond the front line were the Turkish trenches, strongly loopholed and with heavy overhead cover.

I distinctly saw an officer and several men calmly firing from their practically safe retreat, firing at us.

Owing to the conformation of the ground, the Turks had complete command of the whole hillside. From the front-line trench from which we had jumped off, across the cornfield and up to about fifty yards from their trench, the ground rose in a gentle, concave slope. The last fifty yards was steep, almost perpendicular, so that there was scarcely a square yard of the hillside which could not be observed and brought under fire. They had an ideal target and continually raked it with rifle and machine-gun fire and shrapnel. True, our guns from Suvla Bay kept up a bombardment and at times the Turkish fire died down somewhat, but only to burst out again if any of our troops ventured to move. As far as I could see, none of our troops succeeded in crossing the field on my right. I could not see what happened to Brogden, who had advanced on my left.

While I was observing these details, I was continuously debating in my mind what I should do next. I felt I was not properly knocked out and that I ought to be doing something. I could see none of my platoon around, and I rather quailed at the idea of going back across the wheat field to see if I could join what was left of my men. It seemed useless to go forward by myself. What authority could I exert amongst strange troops? To work along to my left seemed to be the best thing to do. But I did not move and I was not sure that I could walk, as my wound had stiffened by now. I felt utterly miserable, utterly ashamed of myself.

The question of what I should do next was however, soon decided for me. Before I had been very long there, I saw Sergeant Henry of Brogden's platoon, running towards me from my left. He flopped down beside me and together we discussed the situation. He had lost touch with his platoon; he knew nothing of the Company. I told him that I had been hit but that I thought I could still carry on. I suggested that perhaps we had better go on together. Just then, he gave a mighty yell. 'I am wounded! My leg is broken', he cried, but he wasn't. A bullet had hit the ground close to him and kicked a stone hard against his shin. He received only a bruise. A moment later, my turn came.

'My God!' I cried, 'I'm hit again', and I smiled at him. I think I was pleased rather than otherwise. I was satisfied that I was properly knocked out this time, for the bullet had drilled a hole through my foot. I knew that I could not be expected to do any more that day and my mind was relieved. I advised Sergeant Henry to look after himself, and a moment later he had disappeared in the direction from which he had come.

After a while, when I again dared to move (for every movement attracted the attention of the Turkish snipers), I removed my boot and, with the assistance of a wounded man lying near me, applied a dressing to my foot. Then I wrapped a puttee around each wound, took off my equipment and piled it in front of my head, stretched myself as flat as I could on my belly and lighted a cigarette, deciding to remain there for the present.

A man with a broken thigh, lying a few yards away from me, called out and asked for a light. I flung him my cigarette. He lighted his and flung mine back to me.

I must have fallen asleep then for I remember nothing further until I awoke about midday. I think that perhaps I had passed out temporarily from loss of blood. And I had a delightful dream. I thought I was a child of about ten and that I was at home in Crinstown in the paddock in front of the house with half a dozen boys and girls of my own age, making daisy chains. I thought that the party in the paddock was the reality and the battle raging about me a dream and, strange to say, a pleasant one. This idea haunted me for many months afterwards and often it appeared to me that my spirit hovered over and gazed at my body as it lay on the scorched hillside of Gallipoli. I thought that in reality I was dead and that I only imagined I was alive.

The delusion was further impressed on me when I met in Dublin, in the following November, one of my platoon. When he saw me he halted, stared at me in amazement, as if he were seeing a ghost, and cried out, 'God, sir, are you alive? We saw your body in the cornfield and thought you were dead.' However he was evidently sufficiently assured I was not a ghost to have the courage to ask me for the price of a drink, and the sight of half a crown in his palm dispelled any further illusions he had on the subject. Not so with me, however, and for a long time I had to avoid the mention or thought of Gallipoli.

When I awoke and came to myself again, it did not take me long to decide to make an attempt to get back. It was evident that the attack had not succeeded. From what I could see, the troops had fallen back. Some, as a matter of fact, were withdrawing at that moment and taking up a position further back. I learned afterwards that the idea of crossing the cornfield had been abandoned after heavy casualties had been suffered by those who, like myself, had tried to cross it.

Anyhow, I decided it was no place for me. A strong desire not to get hit again, a strong desire to escape, sprung to life in my breast. I put my revolver and all the ammunition I had into my pockets, also my compass, slung my water bottle on the hook of my tunic and set out to endeavour to find my way back to the beach.

My first objective was the bank from which we had jumped off. Once there, I guessed, I would be more or less sheltered from the enemy fire. I dared not go straight across the wheat field; it was in full view of the Turkish trenches. It seemed safer to try to work my way to my left, along the edge of the scrub, and this I at once determined to do. Crawling on my hands and knees, I made what progress I could over the hard, stony, sun-scorched ground. Every few yards I went, I was sworn at by the wounded who lay thickly along my path. 'For God's sake keep quiet!' they cried, 'can't you see you are drawing the fire on us?' Others shouted advice, 'You'd better not try to get along there, you'll surely be for it if you do', and again, 'There's a sniper over there, sir, it's not safe', but my determination to get back was too strong. I did not pause till I reached the cover of the trench.

There were some distressing sights along the edge of that scrub. One in particular, a young officer of the East Lancs, impressed me. He was shot through the thigh, his trousers were soaked in blood and he lay helpless behind a tiny mound of earth.

'Can you crawl?' I asked, 'I'm afraid I can't carry you as I've been shot through the foot.'

'No,' he answered, 'my thigh is smashed; I will carry on here as best I can.'

'Carry on here' – the words fell on my ears as a rebuke, though I could not see what useful purpose I could serve by remaining in that particular spot.

I soon reached the end of the scrub but found I was still some fifty yards from the trench. Several voices warned me not to attempt to cross that exposed space. But I was not to be deterred and, jumping to my feet, or to my foot, rather, I hopped across that exposed ground as fast as my one leg could carry me and fell in a heap into the trench.

Here I found myself among 'C' Company, who had been held in reserve, and I felt more at ease. It was evident that the Company had suffered badly. I saw many wounded lying around, calling in vain for the stretcher-bearers and, equally in vain, for a drink of water. I gave my bottle to one of them. He was shot in the abdomen and must have been suffering agonies. There was not much water in the bottle and I don't suppose the man had long to live, nevertheless I felt the better for having tried to help him. I resumed my journey, feeling more justified in myself. My self-respect had been more or less restored.

I proceeded on my way down the hill, sometimes hopping from tree to tree, sometimes crawling on my hands and knees, sometimes sitting down and pushing myself along with my hands. The ground was very difficult, being steep, sprinkled with boulders and covered with small trees. I passed two of the 'C' Company officers, Jock Elliot and Captain Lowrie. 'Lucky Dog!' said Jock to me as I passed, and he smiled with a tired, drawn face. They warned me not to go further. They said the whole back of the hill was enfiladed with Turkish machine guns and that I had better shelter where I was. When I persisted, they told me where I should find the Doc. Before continuing my journey, I cut myself two strong sticks to help me along, but even with their help I found it very hard to make any progress, with one leg out of action.

I followed the dry watercourse, which, I was told, led to the track we had taken when coming up originally. It was full of boulders and very steep. At one place there was a sheer drop of eight or ten feet. It was here I met Levis (2nd Lt, JHB) coming up from the beach with a water-bottle party. He flashed me a smile, his teeth uncannily white in contrast to his dust-begrimed face, called me a lucky dog and offered me a drink of water. How welcome this drink was, even though it tasted strongly of petrol!

That was the last I saw of Levis. He was killed next day while leading the remnants of 'A' Company in a last, desperate, hopeless attempt to stem the attack of the now advancing Turks. And he had already been wounded too, for, I heard afterwards, blood was squelching through the eyeholes of his boot as he rallied his men. Levis had been my particular friend. We had chummed with one another in Trinity in 1912. It was I who gave him the tip to apply to our Colonel for a commission. We had been very intimate and he had often told me of his premonition that he would never return, not by way of conjecture, but as an absolute certainty. He had made the supreme sacrifice for the sake of a forlorn hope. I am proud to have been numbered among his friends. I remember him every Armistice Day, and mourn his loss afresh.

To return to my narrative. I reached the bottom of the hill somehow and by mere luck found myself on the track we had followed on the way up. Of the events that followed I have ever had but a vague recollection. I fell in with a stream of returning wounded. I did not find our own Medical Officer. The track became blocked with pack mules. Most of my fellow travellers sat down on the ground. I scrambled up the steep bank on the left of the track. With my left hand against the slope and a stick in my right, I worked my way round the hill. It was a slow, tiresome task as there was the merest foothold on the hillside, but I managed it and at last reached level ground. I have no recollection of suffering pain or weariness during this struggle but I was obviously reaching the end of my tether, for before I had proceeded half a dozen yards along the flat, I fell. I laughed at my mishap, got to my feet again and pushed on, but in a few seconds I fell again. I then tried to proceed on all fours, but I had gone only a few yards when a young, broad-shouldered Gurkha detached himself from a group of his fellows who were resting in a cleft in the hillside, picked me up and, throwing me across his shoulder, trotted off with me.

I feel at a loss when I try to describe this man's act. It was completely and absolutely outside the range of his duty – it was probably against orders. Besides, he had been in action during the three previous days and had been out of line for only a few hours. Thus he must have been weary, if not in a state of exhaustion as a man of ordinary physique would have been. Yet, in spite of all this, he did not hesitate to come to my assistance. Undoubtedly, he risked his life and I do not think I should have escaped further injury if it had not been for him. I should have been rash to have pursued my way unaided; by that time, parties of Turkish snipers had worked their way round our left flank and commanded with their fire stretches of the route I should have had to take. Moving as slowly as I had to, I should have been an easy target. As it was, in spite of the precautions he took, I received another wound, also in my left leg, when a lump of lead, from a bullet that struck a rock close to me, penetrated my shin bone.

He carried me for over an hour; I generally put it down at two hours. From cover to cover he bore me, now at the double and again more slowly, stooping to take advantage of the shelter here and there afforded by the banks on each side of the track. At each halt, he carefully tucked me under the bank, sat down beside me and nursed my injured member in his lap. It was exceedingly hot, being around one o'clock, and perspiration poured down his face. At one point I was suffering from thirst and indicated this fact to him. He nodded comprehension and pointed to a place further on. Eventually we came to the well he had in mind. I mention it because it illustrated the many risks my rescuer took. The well was situated in the middle of a broad, flat area at the junction of three gullies. It was ominously deserted and there were many bodies lying about. Obviously the Turk had his eye on it. This did not deter my dark friend. Having placed me in a safe place, he took my bottle and made his way towards the well, worming himself along on the flat of his stomach. He was fully five minutes reaching it and as many returning. To me, it seemed as if he would never get back, and what a relief when he eventually succeeded! The water was pure and deliciously cool and how we did enjoy it!

After what I believe to have been about two hours we reached a First Aid Post where we found a doctor and two orderlies. Here he deposited me on the ground. I turned a moment to speak to the doctor and put my hand in my pocket to obtain a sovereign to bestow on my rescuer as a token of my gratitude, but when I turned round again he had gone, he had disappeared. And I did not know his name nor his unit, nor had I even thanked him. This brave lad was out for neither praise nor reward. He did what he thought was his duty and left it at that. May God bless and reward him.

The doctor applied a dressing to my calf but not to my foot, and shortly afterwards two of our own stretcher-bearers came along. They had no stretcher, said it had been broken by a shell, but they offered to help me back to the CCS. I put an arm round the shoulder of each and for a time I hopped along between them merrily enough. There was no longer any danger from snipers – a great relief – but soon we got tired, worn out. We tried every method of progression in turn. Sometimes I hopped between them, sometimes they carried me, and sometimes, to give them a rest, I crawled on all fours. I became so utterly exhausted that time and again I besought them to leave me where I was till morning. Always they encouraged me with the hope that the CCS was round the next bend; another hundred yards or so and we should be there. But turn succeeded turn and yet there was no sign of it. At last I lay down and said I would not budge. They were too weary to further persuade me so we all sat down. I don't know what would have happened if someone had not come along and told us the Field Ambulance was just the other side of the hill, about five minutes walk from where we sat. Thus encouraged, we made one more effort. The information was correct. At last we were in sight of our journey's end. With thankful hearts we struggled over the remaining few yards and reached the camp, as weary a trio as could well be imagined. It was noon when I crawled across the cornfield at Chanuk Bair; it was dusk when the Field Ambulance came into view. You could have walked it in an hour and a half; it took me seven hours to cover the distance. I never want to make another such journey.

Arriving at the ambulance, I was placed on a stretcher and given a cup of tea and soon after dark I was moved nearer the beach and left under a clump of fig trees, where I remained until morning. In the dim light I could see rows of stretchers all around me and the groans of the occupants reached me from all directions. Soon, however, I was asleep, and though I woke a few times during the night, dawn was upon me in what seemed a short space of time.

10 August 1915

As soon as it was fully light, a party of stretcher-bearers began moving us to the Evacuation Point from where the casualties were despatched to the hospital ships which were riding in the Bay of Suvla. It was about a mile distant and, to reach it, a long stretch of exposed beach had to be crossed. We were about half way over when a party of Turkish snipers opened fire on us and thereafter it was a case of advancing by short rushes. Many of the bearers were hit, and not a few of the wounded. When we set out there was a spare bearer to each stretcher but, before an hour had passed, there were not enough to provide two to each, and only the bravest of these dared to keep going. At last an officer came hurrying after us and stopped the procession. I was fortunate enough, as it proved, to be near the head of the column when it halted. Our stretchers were placed under cover of a low sandbank and orders issued that they should be left there until it would again be safe to move on.

At about 10a.m. a party of Indians with pack mules passed along the beach between the line of stretchers and the sea. Snipers opened fire on them, wounding many of the mules. They also attracted the attention of a Turkish battery of guns which forthwith systematically shelled the beach with shrapnel. It began some distance away from me and gradually drew nearer as shell succeeded shell. The strike of each shower of bullets was plainly and painfully visible on the sandy beach or in the sea. There would be a poor chance of escape for anyone on whom it fell. So we thought, as we lay helplessly on our stretchers. Nearer and nearer it came. The last shower of bullets hit the ground

fifty yards from where I lay. Where would the next fall? I
resigned myself to my fate. I thought it was impossible that
I should escape. But the unexpected happened. The next
burst was further away than the last one and the next
further still. Was it possible we had escaped? It seemed
absurd, but it was true enough. In a few moments the
shells were falling away along the beach. They drew further along still and at last they ceased altogether and we
breathed again.

I never discovered what damage was done on the beach
that day. Most of the shrapnel seemed to fall near the sea
and our line of stretchers was about fifty yards up the beach.
But I do know they gave us a bad half hour and one I, at
least, am unlikely to forget.

As the day wore on it became exceedingly hot and,
of course, we had no shade of any kind. I had lost my
pith helmet on the way down and, fearing I should get
sunstroke, I took off my jacket and put it over my head.
This was but poor protection. The burning rays seemed to
penetrate to one's very soul. Anyway they penetrated my
right shin from which I had removed my puttee and used
it to protect my wounded limb. My shin was scorched
most unmercifully and for days it was much more painful
than any of my wounds.

At about noon, I decided I could stick it no longer, or
perhaps the desire to get back again took possession of me.
Anyhow I determined that, since the bearers refused to
move, I would make the attempt myself. And make it I did.
After crawling over the hot sand (and it was burning hot)
for about half an hour, I at last reached the Field Hospital.
The last stage of my journey was under the shelter of the hill
behind which the hospital was hidden and was not exposed
to the Turkish snipers. The Colonel's and Ryan's batmen,
spotting me as I came near the hospital, came forward to
pick me up and carried me into the receiving tent. At last I
had reached the end of my troubles, but as I lay in my tent,
I could not but feel sorry for those still lying on the beach

There was a battery of 4.5s near the hospital and this struck me as being rather an infringement of the Red Cross rules. However, I suppose it could not be avoided on account of the congestion in the narrow hinterland. I nearly came in front of the guns as I came in, and it was only the shouts of the teams that stopped me. As soon as I heard the shouts, I threw myself on the ground, not knowing what the danger was. Then bang! bang! bang!, the four guns went off and I was enveloped in smoke. I considered myself lucky to escape with nothing worse than singing ear.

4

Evacuation

10 August 1915

There were not many wounded in before me so I was attended to almost immediately. My wounds were soon dressed and I was placed in a bell tent with three others and given a drink. After a short time I fell asleep. I awoke about three o'clock and, looking out under the flap of the tent, I saw that everywhere around was covered with stretchers. I just noted the fact and dozed off again. It was growing dusk when I again woke up and, on looking out, I observed that all the stretchers had disappeared. I wondered what this meant and anxiously awaited the advent of someone from whom I could enquire. At length an orderly came in and I asked him.

'Oh, they've been evacuated in the hospital ships', he said, and to further questions he replied, 'No, they're not taking any more off today. The hospital ships are all full.'

This fairly shook me. I did not at all relish the idea of spending another night on the peninsula, and determined I would not, without first making certain the information I was given was correct. So, climbing off my stretcher, I crawled out of the tent to see what could be done. I was lucky enough to meet the two batmen who had already assisted me and, with their help, I got down to the beach.

I found about thirty others, as miserable looking as myself, sitting on a small jetty. The beach was strewn with broken timbers and debris of all kinds, and the jetty badly smashed by shellfire. There was a pile of blankets near the timbers. I sat down and wrapped one of the blankets around my shoulders, having been relieved of my jacket early in the afternoon.

There were a few lighters riding at anchor outside the jetty and further out in the bay a small motor launch dodged about to avoid the shells which some Turkish gunner sent in her direction. The presence of the launch gave us hope, but darkness was closing in and as yet there was no visible sign of anyone coming to take us away. We were growing very anxious and began to fear we should have to spend the night where we were. Then we saw an officer approaching with a party of wounded. This looked like business. In a few minutes he had hailed the commander of the launch, who without much ado, made fast to one of the lighters and towed it over to the jetty. Soon we were all aboard and steaming out into the bay. It was fairly dark, the shelling had ceased and we were on our way to a hospital ship. Now we felt we were out of danger, the nervous strain relaxed, and we began to feel quite cheerful and happy.

The Naval Officer in charge of the launch approached several hospital ships in turn and tried to get us taken aboard but without success. All of them were full up. At length he turned in despair to the skipper of a trawler who, after some hesitation, agreed to take us on board. During this operation, one of the deckhands was wounded by a stray bullet. This was the last Turkish bullet that came near me.

I have little recollection of what happened during this night. I found myself lying on the grating over the hold of the trawler, with several others. It was difficult to keep from rolling off. The night was cold, and as I was dressed in only drill trousers and shirt, I felt it a good deal.

At Imbros, about midnight, we were transferred to a hospital ship. I was one of the last to be taken off the lighter and as I was being helped up the stairs of the ship, I collapsed. As soon as I recovered, I was carried up to the promenade deck and placed on a mattress amongst a lot of other cases. Before they recorded our names, etc., it was discovered that I was an officer and I was placed in a cabin. I had lost my jacket and so had no badge of rank.

There were three officers in the cabin. All of them were in a critical condition. They died during the next twenty-four hours and were replaced by three others.

I shall not forget my first meal aboard. I think it was lunch; somehow we had missed breakfast. I had not had what could be called a meal for six days, and for two days I had had no solid food at all. Still, I did not know I was hungry – until I began to eat. Then it became very evident that I was very hungry indeed. I wolfed everything that was set before me, roast chicken, it was, and then began looking forward to the next meal. This stage did not last long, for, though I did not realise it at the time, I had dysentery. And, very soon after the meal, I became ill and vomited all I had eaten. The dysentery grew worse, there were no attendants, my wounds became inflamed and painful and thereafter I took no more interest in meals or anything else. I just did my best to bear things as they came.

Having reached the harbour of Mudros, we lay there for a few days. Then, one morning, we were wakened with the joyful news that we were to be transferred to the *Aquatania* and brought to England. What good news that was! We had heard that some of the cases were being sent to Lemnos and others to Alexandria. My ticket was marked 'Base' and my wounds were not considered serious. If there was one thing I should have hated it was to have been left at Mudros, that place of hateful, baneful memory, of flies and dust. I rejoiced with exceeding great joy when I learned I was being sent home.

On the *Aquatania* I found myself in a very large cabin with one other patient, a lieutenant in the Manchesters. The cabin might be better described as a stateroom. It had its own toilet and bathroom and a very large window.

The trip home was without incident. We called at Naples to take on coal. Thereafter, a film of coal dust covered the floor. By then, my cabin mate and I were so reduced by pain and sickness that to raise ourselves in our beds and look out of the window was as much as we could do.

'See Naples and die!' says the legend. I think we were both prepared to do so. We viewed Gibraltar in a similar manner. How strange to be so near such sights and not to bother about them. My foot pained me a good deal during the passage. It became frightfully inflamed and I had to keep it in a saline bath all day, rather a tiresome business. Two minor operations were performed on my other wounds, without even a local anaesthetic, and two biggish splinters of lead fished out.

My foot began to look so bad that they thought it was becoming gangrenous and decided that a portion of it would have to be removed. This proposal rather upset me and I awaited the ordeal with fear and trepidation. Luckily for me, the surgeon who was to perform the operation developed blood poisoning in one of his hands and the operation had to be postponed. A consequence of this accident is that my wounded foot is now just as whole and sound as the other one. I was told that the surgeon had 700 patients and I often wondered who took over from him.

The other occupant of our stateroom, the Lieutenant in the Manchesters, was in a much worse state than I was. He had a compound fracture of the thigh and suffered much pain. To add to his troubles, he developed 'prickly heat'. I had my dysentery and was constantly on the go. We were indeed a sorry pair and after a few days were not much to look at.

Lt Pollock paid me a couple of visits during the voyage and gave me some news of the battalion. The Colonel had been wounded in the head and was on board; he bewailed the loss of his battalion from morning to night. Our brigadier was also on board, and Brogden, badly wounded in the shoulder. McGavin also paid me a visit. But mostly I was left alone and my two visitors knew very little of what had happened to the others.

5

Highclere Castle

23 September 1915

The days passed unnoticed and when, on 23 September 1915 (six weeks after evacuation from Gallipoli) I heard we had reached Southampton, I was pleasantly surprised. Then came the disembarkation staff. My companion was marked for Manchester, I for Lady Carnarvon's hospital, Highclere Castle. The stretchers came and in a twinkle we were in the ambulance, ashore. I then saw, for the first time, the dimensions of the *Aquatania*, in all the glory of her 49,000 tons. Then the crowd on the docks caught my eye and I felt ashamed at being exposed to the public gaze when I was in such a sorry condition, followed by a feeling of pleasure that so much interest should be taken in us. A lady came forward with flowers and cigarettes and took my name and home address. She told me she would send a telegram to my mother informing her of my safe arrival. That pleased me. Then, after a few more kind words and a smile that warmed the cockles of my heart, she directed my stretcher to the ambulance intended for me and soon I was part of a convoy and heading for my destination. Cheers rose from the crowds that thronged the docks' approaches as they made way for the convoys and, thus encouraged, we faced the journeys to our respective destinations with smiles on our faces.

My ambulance, after passing through the streets of Southampton, emerged on the north side. How delicious it was to behold, once more, the green fields and long lines of elm trees that bordered the roadside! How different from the yellow, inhospitable, sun-scorched hillsides of Lemnos and Gallipoli! I shall never forget the impression it made on me. The coolness, the shade, the delicious freshness, filled me with delight.

It took us about two hours to reach Highclere Castle. The driver cannot have been an expert; he bumped the ambulance atrociously, and every bump drew a groan from one or other of the four occupants, myself included. My dysentery was preying on my vitals just then and every jolt was a new agony. It was a relief when at last we jolted to a full stop.

Highclere Castle, interior.

Almina, 5th Countess of Carnarvon (1877-1969). She would have been thirty-eight when the photograph was taken.

The Countess of Carnarvon met us at the front door of her beautiful castle and greeted us with the kindest and most welcoming words. By the time we had reached our respective rooms we felt that, in truth, we had come to a haven of rest, to a veritable paradise.

As soon as I had partaken of some refreshment I was taken over by two nurses who then set about the task of getting me clean. I had not had a wash since we had left Naples, where we had taken on coal, and what with the coal dust and the fact that I had no slipper for my good foot, the task was no light one. After being thoroughly scrubbed, I was eau-de-cologned and then powdered and, believe me, I did feel fine when at length they came to the end of their exertions. Later on came Lady Carnarvon and the doctor to inspect my injuries. She did the undressing and later the dressing of my wounds. She told me she was going to nurse me herself, personally. Then I learned that she had decided to take on as her own patient the first Irishman that arrived and I was the lucky man. She, apparently, had a penchant for the Irish and all the nurses and doctors were of that nationality. All the same, I felt highly honoured to have a Countess for my nurse. She was an expert nurse, too, having done two years' training in a hospital. She did everything for me, washed and bathed me, did my dressings, visited me at mealtimes to see that I had everything I required. My foot was a horrid-looking mess and she took infinite care with it. Also she had specialists down from London at the weekend to see it. I had been in hospital many times, but never before had I felt so well looked after. My dysentery bothered me a lot at first and I felt awful at having to turn away the lovely dishes of fruit that came up with my meals. It took me two or three weeks to get the better of it.

A pretty nurse at Highclere Castle Hospital.

I made rapid progress. In a week's time I was being taken out in a bath chair, after another week I was able to get about on crutches. It was then that Glover and my sister Mollie paid me a visit. They were on their honeymoon. Mollie thought I looked like an escaped convict who had been existing on hips and haws for at least a week. My cheeks, she said, were shrunken and hollow, my eyes had a hunted look about them and were bulging out of my head and my hair was standing on end. I looked a miserable specimen. When she called again in a week's time I looked much more respectable, in fact, she was delighted with my progress.

From the time I arrived at Highclere Castle I was charmed with it, but it was only when I came to myself properly and was able to move around that I realised how very beautiful it was. The wide, smooth-shaven lawns with their majestic Lebanon Cedars and groups of tall Scotch Firs swept in graceful undulations from the front of the noble pile of buildings. To wander over the yielding turf or sit beneath the shade of the wide-spreading cedars in the glorious September of 1915 – what better solace could be imagined for those so recently returned from the foul trenches of Flanders or the scorched hillsides of Gallipoli, and certainly they appreciated it. The gardens with their flowers and ripening fruits, their well-stocked greenhouses and conservatories, their winding paths and graceful statues, were another source of delight. And the castle itself – what a noble pile and how well-maintained! All that wealth could give, all that good taste could command was assembled there. The huge library with its countless books and (what was even more in request by us) the deep, luxurious armchairs, was our dayroom, and off it was our dining room where we were given the best of everything. Homemade beer was served at lunch and wine and whiskey at dinner, and a butler and footman waited on us. I don't think any of us could claim to have experienced such luxury hitherto.

A group playing cards at Highclere. David Campbell is seen nearest the camera.

A group of patients at Highclere Castle Hospital.

Lady Carnarvon sometimes brought her daughter Lady Evelyn with her when doing her rounds. She was a girl of about fourteen, I should say, and a very charming person indeed. She also brought Lord Carnarvon in to see me. He was then engaged on his Tutankhamun explorations, though I did not know of them at that time.

The weather must have been exceptionally fine that September for, I remember, we sat out of doors on many afternoons and played card games. We were thus engaged when Mollie and Glover called to see me.

A couple of visits from friends we had made while our Division was encamped at Basingstoke before we embarked for Gallipoli, and a couple of runs to Basingstoke with the same friends in their car, were the only other events that broke the peaceful monotony of my stay at Highclere. Soon, all too soon, the day of my departure arrived, for though I was glad at the thought of getting home, I was loath to leave so divine a place and reluctant to part with my so charming hostess, my so kind and capable nurse. But events in France were proceeding apace. The first great battle of Neuve Chapelle had just been fought. Room must be made for the incoming wounded, so I and three others, all apparently recovered, were ordered to appear before a Medical Board on 4 November 1915. And so, on a Sunday afternoon, I bade farewell to the most delightful place it had ever been my lot to encounter.

My friends from Basingstoke collected me the day before I was due to be boarded, and put me up for the night and, next day, put me on the train for London.

The road to Basingstoke ran through the country over which, during the three months prior to embarking for the East, we had done our divisional training. What poignant memories it called up! Along this very road had marched our battalion, a thousand strong, every officer and man as fit and as tough as hard training and long marches could make him. How proud we were then! How we gloried in our strength, our fitness, our smartness! Some even dreamed of glories to be won, of honours to be gained. And now, what of us? Some had paid the extreme penalty. For them the last post had sounded. Seventy-five per cent were in hospitals, many of them maimed and broken. A remnant were on Gallipoli still but, alas, too few in numbers, too shattered in spirit, to be of any avail or to go into action as a separate unit. How futile all our training, our field days, our reviews. In a few days our grand battalion was shattered, smashed as if it had been a piece of earthenware, wiped out without having achieved anything. Such is the penalty of having taken part in a show that was a failure. To me it seemed, on that day, that life could never be the same again, could never again be worth living.

I stayed the night at Basingstoke with my good friends who were more than kind to me. We were glad to know that those of us who had been their visitors during our training days had all come through, wounded it is true, but still alive. They listened eagerly to the tale of our adventures and misadventures which I had to relate and, though it was anything but a glorious tale, they were full of sympathy and interest.

6

Home on Leave

4 November 1915

At Caxton Hall, I was boarded and given a month's leave.
I then headed for home. On the train to Holyhead, my
foot became rather painful and I had to remove my shoe.
This served as an introduction to two officers and a lady
who shared my carriage. It also drew an apology from
the lady who, in conversation with the two officers who
were proceeding on embarkation leave, had thrown a few
broad hints about young men not joining up, etc. I, being
in mufti, she of course classed me with them. When she
discovered I had just returned from the front, she grace-
fully withdrew her remarks and thereafter was most kind
and considerate.

My foot did not improve during the journey and
when I reached Ardee I was not as hearty as I might have
been. I was met at the station by Mother, Maggie and
Jimmy in a motor car, and conveyed home with much
rejoicing. They were glad to have me home again, safe
and comparatively sound.

I was one of the first in the district 'back from the front'
and, as such, was an object of curiosity to my friends and
neighbours and many a time I had to tell the tale of my
adventures. Our rector showed more real interest than,

perhaps, any of the others and drew me into a more detailed account. 'With a bit of touching-up', he said, 'that could be made into quite a story'. But he never did anything further about it.

Instead of improving, my foot grew steadily worse. It became hard and turned almost black. It was very painful. At last I decided I would have to have it seen to. Thus it came about that, after three weeks exactly, I was admitted as a patient to King George V Hospital in Dublin. I spent four weeks there and enjoyed the stay very much. I was on my feet again in about a fortnight but even before that I was taken out several times to dinner by the chaplain and by other kind folks who did that sort of thing as a duty. There were only four other officer-patients in the hospital at the time and the authorities could afford to be a little extra kind to us. So could the nurses, and they were too! When we were, eventually, able to get around with crutches, we had quite a gay time. It was down town for the theatre, or up to the chaplain's for the evening. His daughter helped to entertain us. Another patient and one of the nurses generally came with me on those visits.

At first, after we became mobile, we used to parade at the Colonel's office to ask leave to dine out, but later we found a better way. The Sister very kindly gave us the key of the back door, and from then on, we came and went as we liked. Formerly we had had to be in by 9.30, now we generally came in time for supper with the night staff, that is, around eleven. Then, in the morning, we had breakfast in bed at 9.30 and just managed to get dressed in time for lunch. This scheme of things suited us fine.

On one of the occasions when I was taken out for a drive, my conductor brought me out through the Phoenix Park and on to the Spa Hotel at Lucan. On our way through the park, he kept on pointing out the various places of interest. Now, while my battalion was stationed in the Royal Barracks in Dublin we had done a lot of our training in the

Park, and I knew 'Each lane and every valley green, Dingle and bushy dell'.

As we drove past the so-familiar places where we had drilled and marched and trained so hard, I could not but remember the battalion as it was then, and the companions I had made, and my own feelings as I tried to learn to be a soldier. Now the battalion was scattered, decimated, its glory departed. Many of my companions of those so recent days I could never see again – their bones were now whitening on the arid hillsides of Gallipoli. The memories were acutely painful. I could have wept. I revealed none of these thoughts to my companion. I just remained silent.

On leaving hospital I of course went home to Crinstown, having been given another month's leave. My foot was now growing stronger and, as soon as I could move comfortably, I paid a round of visits to various friends and relations. I also visited the family of my fellow officer T.W.E. Brogden in Dungannon. It was he who had shouted 'Come on Campbell!' when we made our first charge on Gallipoli. Few of those people had seen anyone 'back from the front' and at that time they displayed a gratifying, flattering interest in me and were eager to hear my story. Perhaps I enjoyed being treated as a hero.

When I returned from the last of these visits, I was met at the station by Amelia, who greeted me by thrusting a telegram into my hand and announced that I was to appear before a Medical Board in Belfast the next day.

When I got home, I wept at the news. This was the end of my leave and it had passed so quickly, and I should have to catch an early train in the morning, and I should have to pack my kit tonight, and I was so tired. And again I wept.

How I hated packing that night. It was awful. I had never worked with so heavy a heart. What did the future hold for me? It was pregnant with possibilities. What would happen to me ere I returned? If I returned? This was so different from my first departure, when I gaily kicked my Greek lexicon in the air and set off on what I thought would be a wonderful adventure. Now I knew what I might expect. Already I could hear the whine of bullets past my ears and the noise of bursting shrapnel over my head.

As I expected, I was passed fit by the Board. I was given two month's light duty and ordered to report to the 4th Irish Rifles at Carrickfergus, forthwith.

I then pleaded for a short respite to enable me to collect my kit from my home, although I actually had my kit with me at the time. They referred me to the adjutant of the battalion and suggested I should phone him. When I did so, he was highly amused. 'The first thing you do when posted to my battalion', he remarked, 'is to ask for leave.' Nevertheless, he granted me the two days I had asked for and home I went, lugging my valise with me.

This respite enabled me to school myself to face the ordeal that lay ahead and to collect my thoughts. And so, having repacked my kit and enjoyed a last round of golf with Elizabeth at Dundalk, I duly reported at Carrickfergus on 4 January 1916.

7

Return to Active Service

Carrickfergus

4 January 1916

It was with some trepidation and a certain amount of nervousness that I approached the Headquarters of the 4th Royal Irish Rifles to report for duty. I guessed that the way of life in this proud reserve battalion would be somewhat different from what I had experienced in the 6th Service Battalion and that a different style of conduct would be called for. I am by nature a bit shy about adapting myself to strange company and I did not relish the ordeal in front of me. However, in the anteroom before dinner on the evening of my arrival, I was fortunate enough to fall in with one Captain Barton, whom I had known before the war. He came forward when he saw me and gave me a warm welcome and then introduced me as an old friend to those near us. A couple of rounds of drinks put us at our ease and I quite enjoyed the occasion. At any rate the ice was broken in a very pleasant manner and the ordeal I had feared was not as bad as I had anticipated.

I found several officers of the 6th Battalion already here. Among them was my old friend Nathan McGavin and also Jock Elliot, whom I had last seen when I was on my way from the front line on Gallipoli. There were many junior officers, few of whom had seen active service abroad. McGavin had palled up with another officer, somewhat senior to himself, I should imagine, and one that cut quite a figure in the Mess and in the clubs and theatres in Belfast. In the circumstances, it was not surprising that he should have no further use for the company of one like me who was rather inclined to take a back seat.

I did not take too kindly to the life there. The Mess was ruled by the Senior Subaltern who was also Mess President. He was a man well in his forties and why he never got promotion was never revealed, nor why he was never sent to the front. He was a stickler for etiquette and discipline in the Mess and nothing gave him more pleasure than to be given the opportunity of telling off some unfortunate who infringed a rule. He did his best to make our lives miserable and we hated and feared him. Of course, we were a pretty raw lot – none of us had been through Sandhurst and few were accustomed to polite society. I remember one particular offender. He had no idea how to behave at the dinner table. He could never remember to place his knife and fork side by side on his plate when he had finished a course, and I have seen the whole Mess 'stand and gaze' while the head waiter was sent to tell him what to do to allow the table to be cleared. The waiters would not touch a thing until everything was in order. Then, there were the irritating fines; on several occasions I was fined 2s 6d for failing to warn 'out' for dinner. On one occasion several of us were fined 5s for using the Mess after 12.15a.m.

I'm afraid we led a frivolous, irresponsible, rakish sort of life. We had practically no duties or responsibilities. We went up to Belfast nearly every night. A typical week in my diary reads:

Monday: stayed in
Tuesday: went to the Hippodrome
Wednesday: stayed in

Thursday: dined in Belfast
Friday: went to the Opera House
Saturday: paid a second visit to the Hippodrome

And so it went on from week to week. Very little effort was made to introduce us to the social life of Carrickfergus. On one occasion, however, several of us were invited out to tea by the Colonel's wife. No doubt an equal number of ladies were present, though I don't remember having noticed any. What I do recollect is sitting on the extreme edge of a sofa, trying to balance a cup of tea in one hand and a brandy snap in the other. The brandy snap was rolled into the form of a cylinder and, when I tried to take a bite off it, it broke into fragments which fell on the carpet at my feet. It was the most embarrassing moment of my life. I did not make a date with any of the female guests nor was I invited to tea a second time in that house.

I can't say I enjoyed my stay of three months at Carrickfergus. I never became part of any cliques. I just knocked around with a bunch of fellows who, like myself, had seen some active service and were bent on making the most of the few weeks they had before returning to the front. We went to clubs and pubs and theatres and dances. Some of us became involved with chorus girls or leading ladies. That I avoided. I played golf a few times and managed to get weekend leave a couple of times when I went home and had a game of golf with Elizabeth.

This frivolous, aimless life came to an end, and quite suddenly. I had already been passed fit and on 15 of March 1916, when I least expected it, I was warned for the front and was given two days embarkation leave. I went home to say goodbye to the folk at Crinstown, had a game of golf with Elizabeth and the McDonalds at Dundalk and returned to Carrickfergus next day. I was just settling down to another round of frivolities when, on a Sunday afternoon, I was called to the orderly room and told I had to report for embarkation at Devonport the following

Home on Leave. David Campbell with family members at Crinstown.

morning. No time for a final spree. The Adjutant had to
drive me to Belfast and put me on the train to Dublin so
that I could catch the mail boat to Holyhead next morning. What a rush, packing my valise and getting it into his
car and then dashing for the station.

On the mail boat I met an officer I knew and, on
reaching London, we went together to an hotel where
I parked my gear. Had I had any sense, I should have
left it at Paddington Station where I proposed to catch
the midnight train for Devonport. After we had dined
at the hotel I found I had a few hours to spare before
my train left, so off I went with my friend to a theatre
show. The Hippodrome, it was, and I noted in my diary
that we saw Gerty Miller there. When we emerged from
the theatre we were met by a blizzard. Already the snow
lay thick on the ground and there wasn't a taxi or cab to
be seen anywhere. Having fought our way through the

blizzard to the hotel, I collected my gear, a great big fat heavy valise, and was faced with the problem of getting it to the nearest tube station. There being no alternative, I set off hauling it behind me over the snow, fear that I should miss my train tugging at my heartstrings. A passing soldier, seeing the trouble I was in, came and offered his help, God bless him, and between us we managed bravely. I couldn't have managed by myself. I learned later that the snow blizzard had caused an hour's delay in the train that followed mine. I also learned a couple of weeks later that I had been lucky to have got through Dublin without being held up (March 1916). Liberty Hall, it was said, was manned by machine guns at the time. (Easter Monday in 1916 was on 24 April.)

On reaching Devonport, I pulled my orders out of my pocket and read them once again. To my horror and disgust, I found I was at my destination twenty-four hours too soon, and I thought of all I could have done with that twenty-four hours – a night in London, or in Dublin, or at home, and all the hurry and scurry and dragging my valise through the streets of London. Well, well, well, wasn't I disgusted!

When I arrived at Devonport, I and several officers were informed that there was no more room in the Embarkation Camp and that we should have to find our own accommodation. We accordingly put up at the Royal Hotel, the nearest place available. We felt a bit sold at the end of our week's stay when told we should have to pay our hotel bills. I knew my account at Cox's was overdrawn. The hotel, however, accepted our cheques; there was little they could do.

The weather this week was just perfect. I fell in with another officer of my own age, an Oxford don, Cannon by name. He was of a different type to those I had been hobnobbing with recently, a man with a philosophy and a non-drinker, and I enjoyed my friendship with him. This was to be his first spell of active service abroad. We spent most of the week at the Hoe in Plymouth, or exploring the coastline along towards Cornwall. There was a delightful restaurant at the Hoe where we had tea almost every afternoon.

We were, of course, on the *qui vive* all the time. Our evenings were often spent at the Royal and Hippodrome; we were enjoying ourselves, though not fully relaxed for always at the back of our minds was the consciousness that at any moment we might receive our embarkation orders. Rumours reached us that the ship that was coming from London to take us on board was delayed by submarine activity in the Channel and had to take shelter at several ports on the way. This was not very reassuring news and was inclined to dampen our enjoyment. After a week under these idyllic conditions our ship did eventually arrive, we embarked and all too soon we were waving goodbye to Devonport and ploughing a zigzag course towards the Bay of Biscay.

I was Officer of the Watch on our first night at sea and I had to keep apart from the others and maintain a lookout. The ship was rolling heavily and the zigzag course added to the discomfort. The presence of an escorting cruiser was a reminder of the lurking danger at hand. The fact that we had to carry our lifebelts all the time was an added reminder. I wondered what my reactions would be if the ship was blown up and I found myself in the sea. I hoped I would not let it be seen how terrified I felt.

Our escort left us when darkness closed in and we were able to relax somewhat. My tour of duty passed without incident, all the same I was glad when my relief took over.

There were some 3,000 troops on board including a large contingent of officers. Many of the latter had seen action abroad and, like myself, were returning to their units having recovered from their wounds. We had no duties or responsibilities and saw little of the NCOs or men on board. Our only concern, therefore, was to find the best and most pleasant means of passing the time. It was the month of April and the weather was fine. I spent the first few days sunning myself on the boat deck. It was just glorious, the clear blue skies, the blue sea, the warm sunshine – in fact, the Mediterranean in April. Then I got into a bridge school. We had morning, afternoon and evening sessions; very foolish, I agree. We should have been much better out in the sunshine.

We arrived in Malta on 11 April 1916 and I went ashore with a few others. We did the sights of Valetta and had lunch at the Osborne Hotel, all very pleasant. We noted the flock of goats delivering milk in the principal street, did some shopping and sent postcards and some presents home and generally enjoyed ourselves. We were back on board again at 3p.m. and left for Alexandria at 6p.m. This leg of the voyage was also without incident though we did have a submarine alarm off Crete, just to keep us from relaxing or thinking we had nothing to fear. During the voyage I had seen a good deal of Lt Cannon, the Oxford don, and had formed a very warm friendship with a Lt Toulmin.

On disembarking, we went into camp at a place called Sidi Bishr, in Egypt. During this operation I became separated from my valise and two very anxious days passed before I recovered it. The camp at Sidi Bishr was along the seashore a mile or so from the tramway terminus and to the east of Alexandria. It was actually in the desert of Sahara and from it the sand stretched away to the horizon.

This mile from the tram terminus to the camp was the scene of many calamities on many a day from about 10p.m. to midnight. It must be remembered that the majority of us were bent on celebrating our reprieve from the firing line, in what we thought was the most appropriate way, and after dining in the city, perhaps 'not wisely but too well', often found ourselves none too sure of our balance when we reached the tram terminus. There were no taxis there to enable one to complete one's journey home – one had to do it on donkey-back. For those like myself who could ride it was just a pleasant trit-trot on a great big Egyptian donkey. For those who couldn't ride it was a hazardous adventure which often ended in disaster. But the sand was soft and a fall or two didn't seem to worry them. There were plenty of boys available to restore them to their seats and, if necessary, hold them there, and all generally managed to reach camp safely.

At the camp we were housed in tents. I had one to myself. It contained a cane bed on which I spread my valise and I was very comfortable and content. The tent was double layered, probably as a protection against the sun but also as a protection from the sand which was always blowing around. Despite the two layers of canvas, the sand came raining through and gradually buried my bed. It also penetrated everything I had. On the second day after my arrival I found myself in command of the details of the 31st Brigade, about a Company strong, and thereafter my days were pretty well occupied with duties. Perhaps I took them too seriously. I don't seem to have had any time for sightseeing. It just did not occur to me. At the camp Mess I met several of the officers I had made friends with on board ship, Toulmin amongst them. In the evening we generally went into the city, had dinner and went to a show, or round to the Sports Club or the Union Club. Occasionally we formed a bunch of three or four.

My days, as I have mentioned, were occupied by duties. One day I was in command of the guards at the Prisoners of War camp and on another I was Captain of the Day at the camp and had to turn out all the guards. On another we did a route march across the desert and practised advancing in short rushes. Then I was ill for a couple of days. Thus the time flew past all too quickly and the inevitable day of our departure arrived.

8

Salonica

April 1916

The order 'Prepare to Embark' appeared on the noticeboard and we knew our reprieve was at an end. That night Toulmin and I dined at the Majestic as the guests of Lt W. Whittome. It was our last fling. On the morrow we embarked for Salonica and we knew not what beyond. We had been just two weeks at Alexandria and I must admit we enjoyed the visit well. Before leaving, I bought a book of Kipling's *Barrack-Room Ballads*. This book, though not the same copy, has been my constant companion to this day, and over the years I have memorised the greater part of it. I brought no other literature with me to Salonica.

I was delighted to find my friend Toulmin amongst those on board. He and I became great friends indeed. We sat together that first night at sea and to mark the occasion (it might have been, and indeed was, our last time together) we decided to share a bottle of sparkling Moselle. But a shock awaited us. We had got about halfway through the bottle and were warming up nicely when, to our consternation, we heard the order, 'Proceed to your lifeboat stations! The ship is being chased by a submarine.'

There was nothing for it but to obey the order. There and then we had to drop our napkins, leave our dinner and our

sparkling Moselle and get up on deck as fast as we could.
Having reached our stations, my friend and I linked arms
and leaned over the ship's rail in the gathering dusk. What
were our thoughts? The wine was still warm within us.
We might be blown sky-high at any moment; that did not
seem to worry us, but we were sorry we had not finished
the sparkling Moselle. As we awaited our fate, word came
round that we had shaken off the submarine in the darkness and we resumed our seats at the table. I don't think we
uttered any thanks or expressed any relief at our escape. We
found that what was left of our dinner was cold and that
what was left of the Moselle had lost its sparkle and we
were just plain annoyed and angry at our little celebration
having been spoiled. We reached Salonica that night without further incident and disembarked on the following day
and on 6 May 1916, I rejoined my battalion after an absence
of almost exactly nine months.

Those nine months had been a tragic period for the 10th
Division, not least for the Rifles, and I was fortunate to have
escaped it. Gallipoli had been abandoned on 9 September
when the last surviving officer of the Rifles, Jock Elliot, was
wounded. The Division was reformed at Mudros where it
had assembled prior to its attack on Gallipoli and in the
early part of 1916 it took part in the abortive expedition
to Serbia. In the retreat from Serbia the troops had suffered
untold hardships. Dressed in summer-weight drill uniform
they had traversed snow-covered mountain defiles and had
encountered blizzards, and with but one blanket a man had
to try to sleep on frozen, windswept hillsides. How any
escaped to tell the tale is almost beyond belief. I am glad
I escaped those experiences.

I was given command of 'A' Company (my original
Company) immediately I rejoined and promoted to the
rank of Captain. The Company, however, did not give me
all that enthusiastic a welcome. The officer I superseded, 2nd
Lt Lucas, had been in command for some eight months and
had built it up from scratch with the drafts which arrived

from time to time from home and elsewhere. The drafts were young conscripts of various nationalities who had received perhaps a couple of months' training. Lucas had changed them into smart young soldiers. He was proud of them and it was obvious that they were devoted to him. He had been looking forward to leading them into action and now, just as such a possibility seemed imminent, I came along and he had to step back into second place. It was hard on him and he felt it deeply. Lucas had been a student at Edinburgh University, a Rhodes Scholar, and had originally come from Australia. He was an altogether outstanding individual and I felt it was quite wrong that I should be placed over him, I who had no claim to outstanding ability of any kind. Little wonder he should be 'fed up' at my arrival on the scene. He always, however, gave me his fullest and most loyal support on all occasions, even to the uttermost when I stood beside him as he lay mortally wounded some six months later.

As I faced my Company for the first time, I was not, as I have said, given a very enthusiastic welcome. Apart from the QMS and the CMS, none of the officers and few, if any, of the NCOs or men were known to me. It was the same in the battalion Mess. Apart from the MO, Adams, the QM and my old friend McGavin, all the officers were strangers to me. The Colonel and the second in command had only recently arrived. I was one of the first of the originals to return. This state of affairs, however, was soon remedied and before long several of the old lot had rejoined us and I found myself once again among old friends and happy and enthusiastic about my work. I was, of course, very pleased about my promotion to the rank of Captain, and I soon got to know my junior officers and to like them. A jolly fine lot they were.

We were at this time encamped in tents in a very pleasant situation up amongst the hills about sixty miles from Salonica. The Bulgar lines, as far as we knew, were fifty or sixty miles away. New drafts were constantly arriving and we had a busy time training and equipping them and generally preparing to move up to the front. Early in June we were issued with mosquito nets and we guessed some new move was afoot. Sure enough, orders came in a day or two and we packed up and set out for the Struma Valley, some fifty miles to the north of Salonica.

Our first day's march brought us across the shoulder of a mountain ridge and, as the men were carrying heavy packs and were not in very good training, we had some trouble in getting them along. On reaching the plain, we bivouacked for the night on what looked like a nice spot near a pond. Little did we know the trouble we were letting ourselves in for. That pond, as soon as darkness fell, became a living mass of frogs, and the row they kicked up! You would have to shout to make yourself heard above the din, and it went on continuously, without a break, till morning. It was torture; no one slept a wink that night.

As we continued our march next day (6 June), the temperature must have climbed well into the eighties. Here is how I describe it in my diary at the time, 'A bloody march, hot as hell. A fearful time getting men along, 27 of ours fell out, sixty of the Leinsters, 80 of the Connaught Rangers, 119 of the Hampshires.' It was said that the Brigadier attacked some of the Rangers with a riding whip. One of them died on the roadside. They called it 'murder'. 'If ever I get the chance', said their Colonel, 'I will make him pay for this.' After that we marched only in the early morning and the cool of the evening. At night we bivouacked just off the road. The ground was very rough and hard, one had to hack it smooth with a trenching tool before one could sleep on it.

After a few days we began to enjoy this sort of life. It was somewhat like a picnic. We did not march every day, and when resting I began to take a little notice of my surroundings. The insect life was marvellous. Crickets were everywhere and often disturbed our rest at night. There was an abundance of butterflies in dazzling colours, and

enormous beetles, like the clockwork ones seen in the
toyshops at Christmas. Then there were the stag beetles that
flew about at night. I remember one hitting me in the face
on one occasion as I rode through a wood; it was about
twice the size of a walnut and the blow hurt. As a Company
Commander I, of course, was mounted. As often as not, my
mount was a mule, but now and again I had a horse for a
spell; this made trekking more enjoyable.

It took us about ten days to reach the River Struma,
which constituted the front line of defence. On arrival, we
took the line from the French. We found it in a somewhat
insanitary condition. At 2a.m. on our first night we heard
volleys of rifle fire and stood to arms expecting an attack,
but nothing materialised. We discovered later that Bulgar
patrols have a habit of firing volleys of half a dozen shots
into the air as they make their rounds. After two days there
we handed over to the 28th Division and moved to other
defensive positions further east along the Struma.

It was at this time that the Salonica Army suffered its
greatest setback. In the months of June and July, when
the greater part of it was operating in the Struma Valley,
it was attacked, not by the Bulgar, but by a far deadlier
enemy, the mosquito. They came in clouds. Of course we
had our nets; they had been issued to us before we left the
base, two foot square to each person. Corps HQ could
not afford more adequate ones. They had squandered the
money allotted for the purpose on elaborate quarters for
themselves, mosquito-proof huts, shower-baths, carpets,
even a swimming pool, so we were told.

The tortures we suffered that summer are beyond
description. I shall never forget how, on our first night,
I lay on the ground, a blanket over my knees which were
bare, my arms, which were also bare, folded across my
chest, trying to cover them and my face with my little
piece of net, while the ping of the attacking mosquitoes
made a continuous din in my ears. It was pure torture.
The Struma Valley had the notorious reputation of being

one of the most malarial areas in Europe. Ninety per cent
of the natives were said to have the disease and it was not
long until our men became infected. They went down like
ninepins and in no time every vehicle in the whole Army
was employed in transporting the cases to the base hospitals. The Army was decimated. Questions were asked about
the affair in the House of Commons and the conduct of
the campaign severely criticised, but I do not think that
the GOC was reduced to the ranks or anything like that.
Our brigade was brought back, what was left of it, to a
campsite some ten kilometres from Salonica during the
last week in July. We hadn't accomplished anything but we
had lost more than three quarters of our strength in officers and men through malaria.

We now found ourselves in a very pleasant campsite and
we were able to sit back and take it easy. I had my Company
HQ under an enormous fig tree. Here I had a table erected
with benches around it and here we had our meals and
bivouacs. The figs were ripe at the time, great, big, black
ones, and often dropped on the table with a plomp. We ate
them with great relish. In front of our Mess lay a vineyard,

Postcard of Salonica (Saloniqua) in 1916.

a couple of acres in extent; the grapes were ripe and we enjoyed them too.

And what of the owners of these vineyards and indeed the inhabitants of the large area of Macedonia between Salonica and the River Struma and between the Struma and the mountain range beyond, over which we fought our battles? All I know is that they had been evacuated. Not a man, not a beast, except an occasional half-starved dog, was to be seen. The crops in the fields, mealies, melons, rye, barley and the fruit in the orchards, grapes, apricots, figs, peaches, now ripe in this month of August, were all unharvested, all abandoned. In the houses and lofts were bundles of tobacco leaves drying under the thatch of the roofs, all, all left behind, and eagerly seized upon by our men. I'm afraid it didn't worry us at the time. We just took it all for granted.

The countryside differed from ours in one principal aspect; there were no isolated farmhouses, all the houses were in closely packed groups, villages irregularly placed round a central square. It was a protective measure; isolated houses would be too vulnerable to attack. It was not all that long since bands of marauders roamed the country. The country was indeed quite undeveloped. Apart from the trunk road to Seres there were no other roads to speak of. We encountered only one sizeable town outside Salonica, Dremiglava. It had streets and shops, now half wrecked and falling into ruins. Farming methods were quite primitive, like those in Mudros, much as they were when St Paul wrote his First Epistle to the Thessalonians (Salonica was formerly known as Thessalonica).

We had settled down in our vineyard and made ourselves quite comfortable before the end of July 1916. By then we had proper mosquito nets. Most of the officers had been struck down by malaria. I think the MO and myself were the only ones that escaped. After four or five weeks they began to trickle back from the base hospitals and early in August we began to organise. This was one of my happiest experiences in the Salonica campaign. I left

the base on 6 September riding at the head of my column
and marched to camp at Kilo 25 on the Seres road. Camps
or halting places had by now been established at points a
day's march apart all the way up to Struma. At these we
found a water supply, latrines, a canteen where we could
draw rations and replenish our supplies, and cooking
facilities. By leaving early in the morning we were able to
finish our day's march by 1p.m., then, having had dinner,
we had the rest of the day in which to laze around and
take in the scenery.

Amongst the spare horses in my column I found a lovely
bay mare, a perfect delight to ride in comparison with my
own mount, a short, stumpy cob, suitable, as I used to say,
for a butcher's cart, but not worthy of the name 'Officer's
Charger'. I used to visit her frequently in the horse lines,
bringing her titbits and stroking her nose, and, before the
march was finished, she used to give me a little whiney
when she saw me coming. I found it very hard to part with
her when we reached our destination. The officers were a
nice lot and were wont to bestow on me the dignity of my
job as Officer Commanding; likewise also the NCOs and
men. We were a happy lot, the weather was fine and we
were a long way from the front line.

On the sixth day of our march we reached brigade
headquarters and I handed over my charges and then
proceeded to my own battalion with a draft of men and
remounts for it too. What was left of the battalion was then
in the front line. Things were fairly quiet though there
was occasional shelling and sniping by the Bulgars. It was
while I was there that I saw our artillery. Every available
gun, I was told, was now on the Struma front line. During
the next couple of weeks we carried out several raids
across the Struma, being ferried over the river by the REs.
These proved quite exhilarating and gave us something to
talk about. By now we were receiving bigger drafts and by
the end of the month were up to about half full strength.
The same could be said of the other divisions, all of which

were now poised on the right bank of the Struma, ready for the general attack now about to be launched.

In our sector the main attack was carried out by the 27th Division and our battalion was allotted the task of guarding their left flank. We crossed the Struma at dawn (it having been bridged in the meantime by the REs) and at first met with little opposition. Then the Company on our right came under fire and their advance was checked. My Company was then sheltering under a high bank and our second in command, Major Graham, who happened to be with me, would not let me proceed further until we made an effort to subdue the hostile fire. There was a field of tall mealies on my left front but straight ahead of me the ground was clear. I had a Company of machine guns with me, so we first got them to rake the mealies with their fire. By then I had climbed to the top of the bank and through my field glasses I spotted the sniping post that was causing the trouble. In a matter of a few seconds I had the machine guns on to it and was watching their fire, from the strike of the bullet, converging on the spot. There was no more fire from that post and we were able to continue our advance unimpeded, but we lost one officer killed, Millar, and two officers wounded, O'Halloran and McQueen, and several other ranks. Millar was a great favourite in the battalion and we deeply mourned his loss.

I now led my Company to the position allotted to me and we dug in and prepared ourselves to receive any counter-attack that might come our way. The Company of machine guns dug in on my right, and beyond them another of our companies joined up with the 27th Division. This Division had as its objective the villages of Zir and Bala. The first waves of their attack were driven back, we were told, and a fierce battle raged throughout the day. The final charge of a Scottish battalion, led by its pipers, won the day. The Bulgars stood up to the rifle fire bravely enough but 'the pibroch thrills, savage and shrill' were more than they could stand and they threw down their arms.

The expected attack on our front came as we were still digging in. It was a most impressive spectacle and it lives in my memory as if it happened only yesterday. The Bulgars came into view in mass formation in line of companies. I could see the officers mounted on their chargers. Now, in 1968, the thought strikes me of Alexander the Great, King of this same Macedonia when, some 2,320 years ago, he overthrew 'Darius good and great'. On they came, line upon line of them. The sight should have struck terror into our hearts but it had the opposite effect, it filled us with exultation and in less than no time we were blazing away at them for all we were worth. So, also, were the machine gunners. At the same time, like a thunder clap, or a thousand thunder claps, our guns opened up. They were massed on our flank, less than a mile away. Never had artillery such a target, a mass of troops closely packed together in full view and at close range. When the smoke of the barrage cleared away we could not see a movement and I don't believe the Bulgars had a chance of firing a shot. They were completely taken by surprise and were just wiped out.

We didn't leave our trenches just then but later in the day a battalion on our left front fell back. They came streaming towards us; they appeared completely demoralised. Then came word that we would be called upon to re-establish the line, and at that dramatic moment the Colonel came towards my Company.

'Forward the Rifles', he cried. 'The Rifles to the rescue', he shouted in most dramatic fashion.

Less dramatically, I got my Company out of our trenches and we began to move forward. We had to work our way through fields of tall mealies. The ground was intersected with ridges and furrows and the going was laborious. We encountered little opposition except from shrapnel fire and we duly established a line behind a bank that ran across our front and engaged the enemy with rifle and machine-gun fire until we drove them off.

Coming to our firing line I was accompanied by Major Graham. He had his orderly with him and I my batman. They followed two or three paces behind us. We were facing a certain amount of rifle fire. We heard a yell from my batman as he fell to the ground, and the Major's orderly was hit. We should have dropped to the ground and taken cover but we didn't, we just leaned on our chinstraps and grimly pushed on till we reached the bank where my men had formed a firing line. Later we found that my batman was shot through the thigh; the orderly was shot through the stomach and died later. Having joined my men, I managed to get hold of a rifle. We didn't have much of a target but there was some opposing rifle fire and occasionally we spotted a movement. I don't believe I hit anybody but I found satisfaction in blazing away like those around me. Ever and anon the 'Great Coal Boxes', as we called them, came over. They were falling short of where we lay but we could see the spread of shrapnel bullets as they struck the ground; each burst covered an area about the size of a tennis court.

Darkness now began to fall and we were considering how we should spend the night when, unaccountably, we got the order to retire. It occurred to us that 'someone had blundered', but 'ours not to make reply, ours not to reason why', and back we went over that weary half mile of mealie fields. We kept our men in open order lest one of those 'coal boxes' should burst over our heads, but we didn't escape. One of them did find its target and nearly wiped out Montgomery's platoon. We spent most of the night bringing in our casualties (there were twenty-two in my Company) and reorganising the platoons. Then, as if that weren't enough, just as we began to settle down, we received orders to go back again immediately to the line we had just abandoned. The night was now fairly quiet, though the Bulgars were still sending over an occasional shell. We moved back into position without opposition and settled down to rest, having been on the go for the three previous nights and days. By the next day the Bulgars had disappeared beyond the horizon; there was no follow-up, why, we never knew. We spent the next week or so burying their dead (they had suffered very heavy casualties) and collecting the equipment they had left behind on the battlefield. Then we set to work on a new line of defence, which we took over from the Royal Dublin Fusiliers, and about making ourselves comfortable.

10 October 1916

The line of defence we took over from the Royal Dublin Fusiliers consisted of a system of trenches and dugouts along the Seres road, on the outskirts of the village of Jenokoj. This was a sizeable village and, though it had been heavily shelled, many of the houses were habitable. The men slept in the dugouts but the officers were able to find accommodation in the houses. We had a nice Company Mess in one of the larger houses. Here, for the first time in months we were able to sit round a table for meals and to enjoy each other's company in between times. We had been receiving reinforcements recently and I now had ten officers in my Company. They were: Lucas; Vine; Clapham; Montgomery; Hadden; Rankin; O'Reilly; Moss; Strange, and myself. They were as nice a lot of young men as I have ever met. They were gifted too. Lucas was our intellectual, Strange was a violinist and often played for us. Vine was an architect and O'Reilly, our latest acquisition, was the most friendly and cheerful soul you could meet on a day's march. Years after the war I happened to meet him on the street in Dublin.

'I shall never never forget the welcome you gave me when I joined your Company', he told me. 'How d'you do, what'll you have to drink?', were my words of greeting, he said. I had treated him so nicely and was so friendly that he loved to recall the occasion. It lives in my memory too. His friendly smile won my heart on the spot. Referring to these times, Lucas, in a letter to his father, wrote, 'In the

Company here we are a very happy family'. This appears in a book entitled *The Life and Letters of Norman Carey Lucas*, written by his father, who sent me a copy. I am glad to have seen these words – Lucas must have had some hard feelings about me when I took over the command of 'A' Company from him six months before. We were, indeed, a very happy family and during the next couple of weeks, although our lines were shelled occasionally, we enjoyed the respite and improved our acquaintance with one another.

During this spell we had a visit from the Crown Prince of Serbia. I remember how we collected a lot of scrap and spread it around some shell holes and showed it to the prince, telling it was a particularly 'hot spot'. We also had a visit from General Briggs, commanding the 16th Corps, who decorated those who had received awards in connection with the recent engagements. Two of our men were awarded Military Medals. At this time, also, officers were invited to volunteer for transfer to the Royal Flying Corps. Several did, and were accepted, including my friend from Dungannon, T.W.E. Brogden. I was sorry we lost him, though not just then.

Our respite was soon to come to an end; our happy family was soon to be broken up. On 26 October a general advance was being planned. Our brigade, the 29th, was to be allotted the task of making good the ground on the right of the line and our battalion the task of seizing and holding a line of trees called 'Patrol Wood'. The attack was to take place on 31 October. A couple of days before, I was called to the office of the CO and told that my Company would lead the attack. The other OCs and I, accompanied by the CO, rode over to a point from where we could see the objective. Next day I showed the objective to my platoon commanders. At the battalion conference preceding the stunt I asked, 'What shall I do with my supernumerary officers?' On raising the question at the brigade conference, the CO was told by Brigadier General Vandeleur, 'Put them in the firing line. Good training for them.'

On Sunday 29 October 1916 we attended Divine
Service, but fighting had already broken out in some parts
of the line and the noise of the hostile activity drowned the
Padre's voice and we could hardly hear him. Next evening
we moved into our 'jumping-off' position and lay down for
the night. We had our greatcoats but not our groundsheets
and it rained throughout the night and we were soaked to
the marrow. I can remember the sound of the rain on my
steel helmet which I used to cover my face. As we paraded
next morning in our wet clothes we felt cold and miserable
and in no mood for heroic deeds. Nevertheless, by 9a.m.
we had formed up and were moving forward. We advanced
in open order in two waves across the 2,000 yards or so of
open ground that separated us from our objective, our feet
sinking in the soft mud caused by the previous night's rain.

The first wave had almost reached its objective when
it came under scattered rifle fire. Then, with a crash as of
thunder, the enemy artillery opened up. So intense was
the barrage and so dense the clouds of smoke created
that those in the front wave were completely lost to the
view of those in the second wave. But there was no hesitation in the ranks of the latter. On it came, as steady
as if on parade, until it, too was enveloped in that pall of
smoke, in that hell of bursting shells. Those who watched
the advance, and they included our CO and two Generals,
described it as 'magnificent'.

Just before I reached the leading line, I encountered my
second in command, Lt Lucas. He was lying on the ground,
mortally wounded. An NCO was attending to him and
I stayed with him but a minute or two. When I reached
the front line I found the first wave digging in with their
entrenching tools and I went along getting the second wave
into the best position I could find. At the end of the line
I found the Lewis Gun Section all of a heap, lying on top of
each other. Underneath was their officer, Lt Moss. He was
just riddled with bullets and died shortly afterwards. Some
of the others were also wounded and, amazingly, some

unhurt, just scared stiff. On my way back I learned that two
others of my officers had been wounded and evacuated.
They were Lts Vine and Montgomery. Then I encountered
what was perhaps the most distressing sight I have ever witnessed. Lying across the parapet of the trench was a Sergeant
and across his shoulders an officer lay. They were both dead.
I removed the officer's helmet to see who he was and found
his brains filling the helmet. He was Lt Strange, the officer
who above all the others I had allowed myself to regard
with deep affection. The other was Sergeant Campbell
whom I had known since I had joined the battalion in
Fermoy. I myself seemed to have led a charmed life that day.
I was up and down the line many times. When I went to
one end, the other was shelled, when I came back, the place
I had just left came under fire.

Around midday, the shelling eased off somewhat and
I had a visit from the CO who made what arrangements he
could for the evacuation of the casualties we were suffering
and talked about pulling back. He decided, however, that
we should hang on. He stayed with us for about half an
hour. Lt Clapham, my only surviving officer, had his steel
helmet hit by a bullet early on in the day and was a bit
shaken, but he stayed on and saved me from being quite on
my own. I was glad to have his company and his help.

Halfway through the afternoon the shelling ceased and
we were able to get our casualties evacuated. Then, at 1830
hours, as it was growing dark, we got the order to return. We
had done our job of diverting a portion of the enemy forces
from the main attack, which was taking place a couple of
miles to our left and which succeeded in capturing several
important enemy positions and there was nothing left for
us to do.

Back we came, laboriously plodding through the soft
mud in which our boots stuck, and halted at the place
where we had spent the previous night. Doubtless the
Company cooks had a hot meal ready for us; they, of
course, would have stayed behind, but I don't remember

having anything to eat. As I was selecting a place to lie down, I encountered McGavin, who was attached to the battalion HQ for the day and we had a few words. We would have given all we possessed for a swig at a bottle of whiskey but, alas, there was none to be had. As we lay down on the wet ground we huddled together for warmth. When we got up in the morning, our coats were frozen stiff. I often wonder how we endured the cold that night and lived to tell the tale.

We were a sorry-looking lot as we marched back to our trenches at Jenokoj that morning. As we neared our destination the CO rode along the column exclaiming, 'Well done "A" Company.' Later in the day General Langley and Brigadier General Vandeleur personally congratulated my Company. The CO had risen from a bed of sickness to be present at the action and he was awarded the DSO. Major Graham, the MO, and I were awarded Military Crosses. Cpl McIlvenny, who attended Lucas when he was wounded, was awarded a Military Medal. I, and I expect others, were mentioned in despatches as well. We knew nothing of these awards, of course, until nine months later, but I mention them here because they were made in connection with services rendered in the events I have just described. I was, naturally, very pleased to hear the CO's 'Well done "A" Company', but I was too distressed, too woebegone to feel any glow of satisfaction. I was also pleased that the two Generals, who had witnessed the action, went to the trouble to visit our lines and to congratulate my men on their behaviour.

We were glad to get back to our dugouts at Jenikoj and to get into dry clothes and have a decent meal. But our first evening in the Mess was very sad. There were just two of us, O'Reilly and myself, where a couple of days ago there had been eight, the happiest little family you could imagine. Lucas was on his deathbed. Strange, with whom I had formed so deep a friendship, was dead. Moss was dead. Vine and Montgomery were in hospital, severely wounded. Clapham had not yet recovered from having his steel helmet struck by a bullet. Never again would we gather round the same table, never again would we share the hardship of a campaign, and never again, I thought, would I allow myself to regard my fellow officers with affection. In future, I thought, I would harden my heart against the formation of any close friendships. O'Reilly had not accompanied us into action. He had remained at battalion HQ as Liaison Officer. Still, he too mourned the loss of our good friends, as indeed everyone in the battalion mourned their loss.

This was the last major action at which I was present and I reckon it was the saddest day of my life. It is the day that occupies my mind when I stand to attention during the two-minute silence at the Memorial Service on Armistice Day. I often wonder how a fellow like me was spared whereas a man like Norman Carey Lucas, who possessed such vast resources of intellect and character, was taken. Now, fifty-two years after the event, I am still wondering; but such are the ways of Providence, one is taken and the other left and it is not ours to reason why. Although this was the last major action at which I was present it was by no means the last occasion I ran a risk of becoming a casualty, for, after all, one's life is always in danger when there are bullets and shells flying around.

At the brigade conference which was held after the action by the Brigadier, the Brigadier asked our CO to explain why I had so many officers with me on that day and when the question was put to me by the CO I was glad to be in a position to remind him of the Brigadier's words when the same question was raised at the preliminary conference on 29 October. 'Put them in the firing line. Good training for them', he had said. He must have regretted those words afterwards. To us it appeared a futile waste of precious lives and we felt very sore about it. We also remembered that it was he who had taken his whip to a man who had fallen out from exhaustion on a certain route march.

After these events we moved back across the Struma and occupied various lines of defence. Around Christmas we were again north of the Struma and at a large village where we were able to find habitable houses. Here the companies took it in turn to man the outpost lines. One of the posts was a mile or so in front of the main line near a village called Prosenick, and a few hundred yards further ahead we had an advance post which was held at night by an officer and twenty men. The silence of the night was seldom broken but occasionally a Bulgar patrol made its presence felt by loosing off volleys of rifle fire. This happened on a night when 2nd Lt G. was on duty. As volley succeeded volley, each nearer his post than the last, he just got the wind up and bolted, leaving his men to look after themselves. As soon as I heard of the occurrence I sent another officer out to investigate and report. Having reassured the men, he came back and reported to me and I sent out a party to relieve the one the officer had deserted. In the meantime I had phoned the Adjutant and told him what had happened. He, having been wakened out of his sleep, thought he should take further action and allerted the Artillery. All this happened at about one or two o'clock in the morning and as nothing transpired by way of an attack, much annoyance was felt by all those whose night's rest had been disturbed.

Next day I received a long questionnaire from the CO who wanted material for his report to brigade. He had verbally approved of the action I had taken. He made detailed enquiries about the officer concerned and requested a report on him. I couldn't avoid giving an adverse report. As a matter of fact, this officer had been a thorn in my side ever since he had joined my Company. He was never done grousing. He complained about the food, about the running of the Mess, about the mud, the weather – nothing was good enough for him. I remember the words I used. 'This officer', I wrote, 'is not only negatively useless to me, he is a positive hindrance to my Company.' He was the son of a well-known tobacco manufacturer whose chief brand bore his name. Nevertheless, he was sent home in disgrace. In discussing my report afterwards, Major Graham remarked, 'I never knew Campbell had a literary turn'! The 'negative' and 'positive' had taken his fancy.

For about six weeks in December and January we were isolated by floods and only pack transport could get through. No Christmas mail, no turkey, no food but bully and biscuits. Nothing but rain and slush and snow. During this period and for a while later, a feeling of profound boredom prevailed amongst us. This was due not only to the terrible monotony of our work, but also what appeared to us to be its utter futility. We were suffering hardships in plenty but seemed to be achieving absolutely nothing. Those who had malaria were now having relapses and if there is anything more disheartening or more liable to give rise to fits of despair I have still to meet it. Suicides were not uncommon. Our Adjutant went off to Salonica with malaria and shot himself; our Signals Officer had a nervous breakdown; one of our Company Commanders was sent off in the DTs; many of the men reported sick. A similar state of affairs prevailed in the other battalions of our brigade. One of the Colonels, who had a grudge against the Brigadier, promptly put him under arrest one day and placed an officer's guard over him. This Colonel went quite mad and had to be sent home. And so it went on. I can remember the outstanding cases.

On 4 February 1917 we were again back in Kalendra and took over an outpost line from the Connaught Rangers. This was one of my most unpleasant assignments. The line lay across a wide expanse of flooded ground. The trenches were full to the brim with water; the dugouts were full to their roofs. All we could do was to bivouac on the occasional patches of dry ground that appeared above the floods. The weather was bitterly cold. Next day we were issued with thigh-length gum boots and we began preparing a new line defence. We were visible to the Bulgars and they sent over about a dozen shells and we suffered some casualties. By the third day the men's feet were in pretty bad shape from the cold and dampness. It was impossible to dry anything.

On the fourth day it began to rain about 10a.m. and continued throughout the night. Clouds of wild geese, wild duck, teal, etc., filled the sky and alighted on the floods. The noise they made drowned every other sound. We turned machine guns on them as they flew past, but never a one was brought down. The Bulgars sniped at any moving object. Snow and wind heralded in the fifth day and added to our misery. Two miserable-looking Turks, starving, ragged and wet to the skin, gave themselves up. We gave them food which they devoured ravenously. Two men were down with frostbite and many were suffering from trench feet. We held a foot inspection every morning to make sure that the men took off their boots for a while and gave their feet a chance to dry. My orderly, who accompanied me on my rounds, and my batman, who remained behind in my bivouac, escaped the inspections. It was they who got the frostbite, and nearly got me the sack. To contract frostbite was a punishable crime.

On the sixth day I returned to Jenikoj, having been relieved on the previous night by Captain T.W.E. Brogden and 'B' Company. It was a blessed release from a most unhappy position.

After a couple of weeks in Jenikoj we were back again at Kalendra outpost (22 February 1917). By now the floods had disappeared and the weather had improved. We had bad luck on this occasion, however, for, while sitting in our Company Mess shelter, two of my officers, Arnold and Sharkie, were severely wounded by a shell which burst right in the shelter. I have no recollection of Arnold, but I remember Sharkie as a very fine officer. He had been with me only two weeks when he got hit. He rejoined my Company again when he recovered from his wounds.

We now moved back across the Struma into reserve and were given a couple of weeks respite from work, which we appreciated very much. We had an opportunity of meeting our fellow officers in the other companies and in various other units. We gave small dinner parties in turn and sometimes card parties. I remember well coming home from one of these parties. There were three of us and no doubt we were feeling happily exhilarated after the hospitality we had received. We were mounted and, as there were no roads or even tracks, we had to proceed across country. Some of the fields we had to cross had recently been cultivated and were rough and ridged; nevertheless, nothing would do but that we should go at a nice, round gallop. This would have been dangerous enough by daylight but by night, even though the moon was up, it was positively foolhardy. We had to ford a stream perhaps a couple of feet deep and about ten yards wide. We should have walked our horses quietly across but no, we splashed across at full speed and, though we did arrive home safely, we might easily have, like Tam o' Shanter, 'Bought the joys too dear'.

At this time my charger was a very handsome mule, built like a racehorse and with a delightfully smooth action. He could jump, too. One day, cantering across country I encountered the main Ceres road, which had a bank and a ditch on both sides. My mount did not hesitate, just jumped the ditch on one side, cantered across the road and jumped the ditch on the other side. Unfortunately I had failed to notice a telephone cable carried on poles along the side of the road. It caught me under the nose as I jumped; back I went on my mount's tail and nearly came off. I got the hell of a fright though I managed to recover without falling off. If the cable had caught me under the chin I might not be here to tell the tale.

During the next two or three months we manned outpost positions at various villages on the Struma Plain. Sometimes we were able to find sleeping quarters in the houses but as often as not we had to sleep in dugouts. On one of the latter occasions, after sleeping in my dugout for some days and having only a groundsheet between me and the damp earth, my batman acquired a door and fixed it up for me to sleep on. I found this a most delightful change, and when, later, he filled some sandbags with dried grass and laid them on the door, I found this was comfort indeed; I wouldn't swap it for a spring mattress. We were inclined to disregard the sources from which acquisitions such as the door were made until one day our Company cook, when trying to pull some wood for his cookhouse fire from the roof of a house, pulled the whole roof down on top of himself and broke nearly every bone in his body. This incident was made the subject of a court of inquiry and, thereafter, interference with the houses in the villages we occupied was treated as a crime. The injured cook survived but never again will he play as centre half on the Rifles soccer team.

As a matter of fact, nearly all the houses we encountered were in ruins; they were little more than mud huts and their roofs consisted of thatch overlaid with small tiles. We gave little thought to the hardships of the owners when they were forced to leave them and to leave the little bits of farms from which they scraped a precarious living, nor did we worry about the additional hardships they would suffer when, eventually, they would return and resume possession of their tumbledown homes and neglected farms.

Dogs left behind by the villagers when they were forced to evacuate their homes were often encountered hunting in packs and were quite a menace. It was considered inadvisable for anyone to go abroad alone as a pack was liable to attack a solitary individual. Shooting parties were organised to deal with the dogs and I remember an occasion when Brogden led one such party of officers to a nearby village and succeeded in wiping out quite a large number. They enjoyed, as they said, an excellent day's shooting.

Sporting shooting of dogs was not, however, encouraged. Our Colonel and the Major, when paying me a visit at an outlying post one day, got the fright of their lives when they almost ran into a fusillade of rifle fire. They thought an enemy attack was surely developing and when they found that the shooting came from my Company cook who had opened fire on a pack of dogs attracted to the cookhouse by the appetising smells, they were exceedingly annoyed. Strict orders to avert the recurrence of such an incident had to be issued forthwith and I was not allowed to go scot-free either. I had to bear the blame. I bagged a dog myself one day. Returning from a visit to one of my platoons, accompanied by an orderly, I saw a big dog trotting along in our direction and, taking my orderly's rifle, I let fly at it and was lucky enough to bring it down. As it was not quite dead, and to 'ease it out of its pain, I finished it off with my revolver. Poor thing, I hated doing it.

I should like to record here that the famous Michael O'Leary, VC, was posted to my Company on 18 April and remained with me for a few weeks. He had taken part in recruiting campaigns in Ireland and his picture and an account of his heroic deeds appeared on posters all over the country. We were glad to have him but were at a loss as to how to employ him. He had a habit of going on lone patrols and sometimes stayed away for days and filled us with alarm for his safety.

While we were still on the plain, we made a reconnaissance of a line of defence on the crest of a hill south of the Struma which we were to occupy in the near future. It was thought that perhaps the higher ground would be healthier for us during the hot summer months. We were a party of seven mounted officers. We set out at dawn and, after riding all day, returned at dusk. It was quite an endurance test for even the most accomplished horseman amongst us, but for the less accomplished it was quite an excruciating ordeal and they and their mounts suffered severely. Their horses were galled at the withers and were limping before we reached home and indeed were confined to the sick lines for quite a while afterwards. The riders (there were three of them) were doubtless galled too and took many days to recover. My stumpy little butcher's-cart-type charger came through the ordeal without turning a hair and I did likewise. It just shows how severe on his mount an unskilled horseman can be. I could ride before going into the Army and I took advantage of every opportunity that came my way of going through riding school. I therefore regarded myself as a good horseman. Before this episode I was inclined to despise my mount, but never again, and I had several opportunities of demonstrating that the pair of us could outlast even the best of our rivals.

After a few minor engagements during the early months of the summer we came back to the ridge of high ground referred to in the previous paragraph and set about constructing a series of redoubts. Each Company was given about two miles of line to defend. I constructed four redoubts in my section, one of which was a mile and a half in front of the others. Each redoubt consisted of a system of trenches and dugouts. My Company HQ was in the central position and on this occasion I had a tent to myself and a trestle bed of sorts. We also had a Mess tent in which my platoon commanders were able to join me for meals. This was a luxury indeed. The enemy were miles away and we never had any thought of an attack developing. We were able to relax and, though I visited each of my outposts a couple of times a week and tried to maintain a strict state of alertness, it was not easy as there was no apparent reason for it.

Our occupation of this line was practically without incident but there was one event which I shall never forget. The position selected for forward platoon was well down the hillside near the bottom of the slope. The whole area was overgrown with scrub and bushes about ten feet high. There were patches of fairly clear ground and of these we selected the one that would afford the best field of fire. There was nothing we could do on the first day and when we had selected the positions of the trenches, the cookhouse and the latrines, we just set the men to clear the sites for their bivouacs and generally prepare to settle in for the night. It was late in the evening when I returned to my HQ with my CSM. Next day, when I again visited the post, I met a sight which still sticks in my memory. It was that of the men's faces. So swollen and red, they were that I could scarcely recognise them. They had been attacked by mosquitoes during the night and almost eaten alive. They must have suffered agonies. We did what we could to mitigate the trouble by supplying the men with additional nets and repellents, and by lighting bonfires all over the site we endeavoured to clear the immediate vicinity of those deadly enemies. It was a day and an assignment to be remembered.

June had now arrived and during the whole of this month and the month of July we occupied this hill position with little to distract us. We were able to relax and to make social contacts with the officers in the other Companies and the adjacent battalions.

And now I come to the last act in this drama of my experiences with the Salonica Army.

Early in the year, in May 1917 I think it was, by which time most of us were in rags, more or less, I got a notion that I should like some new clothes, so I wrote to my tailor in Dame Street, Dublin, who had made my first uniform, and ordered a complete new outfit: tunic; slacks; breeches; boots and leggings; shirts and underclothes, and a cap. My order was fulfilled in due course and the sizes proved satisfactory. When I turned out all dressed up in my finery, the eyes of the other officers of the battalion almost popped out of their heads. They got the shock of their lives and were filled with envy. I was now the best-dressed officer in the brigade and it was for this reason, I imagine, and maybe because I was wearing the ribbon of the Military Cross, that I was selected to command a Guard of Honour at the presentation of medals by the Corps Commander, General Briggs. The guard was to consist of two platoons from each of the four battalions in the 29th Brigade together with contingents from the Artillery and the Engineers. We were given a couple of weeks to prepare for the event and, having selected my lot, I took the men out of the trenches and submitted them to an intensive course of drill and rifle exercises and did everything possible by way of 'spit and polish' to smarten up their appearance.

It was a good day's march to the scene of the parade, fifteen or twenty miles, perhaps, and as I set out at the head of my column, I felt it good to be alive. The sun was shining, the early morning air was fresh and cool, and our route lay along the crest of a ridge of hills with fine views on either side. We were all in the best of form and glad to get away from the routine of trench duty. I enjoyed that march. I was proud at having been selected for the duty of commanding the Guard of Honour and felt quite exhilarated. We arrived at our destination about an hour before dusk and found we had been allotted a most delightful site on which to pitch our bivouacs for the night. It was an apricot orchard and the apricots were ripe for picking. They were delicious and we did enjoy them. There were also various farmhouses around in which the Staff Officers, etc., were able to find accommodation. The owners had been evacuated perhaps a year previously.

Next morning, about an hour before the presentation, I had various contingents formed up in a hollow square and put them through the drill. I was in good voice and the parade ground, being surrounded by tall trees, gave it resonance and my words of command rang clear as a bell. On the arrival of General Briggs we presented arms and he took the salute. We then stood to attention while he decorated the heroes. The latter then formed up and we presented arms to them. That ended the parade. Everything had gone smoothly and the movements had been executed smartly. Compliments in abundance were paid to all concerned. The contingents then returned to their bivouacs.

9

Back to Hospital

August 1917

I was thirty years old.

I had breakfast, dinner and tea with the brigade staff that day. Next day we marched back to our outpost line and three days later I reported sick. That was 8 August 1917, two years exactly after I went into action for the first time, in Gallipoli, and three years after I became an officer.

Thus ended my service with the 6th Royal Irish Rifles. It was a sad day for me and it was with the greatest regret that I parted from my Company, which I had been so proud to command. It was with sorrowful heart that I said goodbye to my friends and companions with whom I had served through thick and thin, through good times and bad, all through those three adventurous years.

Instead of lamenting my departure I should, perhaps have welcomed it with gladness, so said one of my colleagues. 'Lucky dog', some declared when they heard I was being evacuated, 'Wish I could get away too.' As it turned out, perhaps I was lucky, for a few weeks after I left and while I was still in hospital there, the battalion passed through Salonica on its way to Palestine. Later on it moved to France in time to take part in the Retreat in March 1918. Both these assignments were tough ones and involved the battalion in heavy casualties. Indeed, when it got to France, it no longer functioned as a unit but was split up and used to fill gaps in other Rifle battalions. So it happens that if I had not gone sick, the likelihood is that I should have been exposed to many another hazard to life and limb. So, after all, therefore, it seems I was lucky, or even very lucky.

There was no send-off party for me the night before I left. There never is on such occasions. Nor did I go round and bid goodbye to my Officers, NCOs and other ranks. I seem to have just slunk away like a wounded beast in the forest. As a matter of fact I do not remember anything about it. And my diary just records that I left the battalion on 8 August and went to the 32nd Field Ambulance labelled 'Neuritis'. And so it was that I stepped down and someone else stepped up into my place and was promoted Captain and was given command of my Company. The likelihood is that he threw a party to celebrate his promotion.

A couplet from a ballad that appeared in the *Illustrated London News* during the Boer War springs to my memory now. It ran:

Bugler Dunne, Bugler Dunne
You are missing all the fun
And another boy's been bugling
Where the battle's being won.

But I don't think it occurred to me as I rode off to the Field Ambulance accompanied by a mounted orderly, leading a pack mule with my kit strapped on its back.

On the way to Salonica, I spent nights at various Field Ambulances, by now established along the Seres road. I noted how nice it was to see a feminine face again and to speak to one of the opposite sex. I had not done so since leaving Belfast, a year and five months ago.

At one of the ambulances I met a first cousin of mine, Colonel Pat Henderson. He was a regular RAMC officer and was ADMS to the Corps, operating in Macedonia, the 52nd. I remember how he told me that less than one in ninety of the troops in the Corps escaped contracting malaria. I, of course, was one of those. I also remember how he described the partridge shooting he sometimes enjoyed with General Briggs and members of the Corps HQ staff. Partridges were very plentiful in Macedonia that year because the farmers had been evacuated before they had had time to harvest their grain crops. I remember the General on one occasion. When I saw him he was mounted on a beautiful bay thoroughbred and was cantering across a field of ripe corn, followed by a couple of staff officers and with a pair of Irish wolfhounds chasing along in front of him. Did I envy him? Not 'arf. And did I weep for the poor farmers who had left their crops unharvested? I don't think so. Their fate didn't worry me just then.

Eventually, having been on the move for eight days, I arrived at the 42nd General Hospital, Salonica. It was a very large, red-brick building, furnished, I presume, with every modern convenience.

In the bed on the opposite side of my ward lay an officer of whom I was to see a great deal during my progress towards England. He was Lt Leonard of the Buffs. He was suffering from a broken neck which he sustained when he hit his head against a concealed rock when he was taking a dive at a bathing place a few days previously. The wonder is that his spinal cord had not been severed. He had to lie on the flat of his back and keep perfectly still. The orders were that he should not be moved on any account. Then occurred the great fire of Salonica. The whole centre, the business quarter, of the city was gutted and as it spread towards the hospital, fears for the safety of the hospital were entertained and as a precaution orders were issued to evacuate the patients. I was sent to

the 42nd General, a hospital housed in tents and run by
Australians. When they came to Leonard, the authorities
were faced with quite a dilemma. It was improbable that
he would survive being moved. If they left him and the
fire reached the hospital he would go up in flames. They
decided to risk the latter alternative and as it happened
the fire did not reach the hospital and he survived to tell
the tale of the dilemma.

Very little notice was taken of my case when I arrived
in the 42nd. I was labelled 'Neuritis' and no one bothered
to query the diagnosis. Day after day however the arm
became more painful. I see from my diary that I even
contemplated taking a dive out of one of the third-storey
windows and ending it all. It was all my own fault. I did
not make enough fuss about it. At last, when I could
no longer bear the pain, I did make a fuss. One night I
pulled down my mosquito curtain and wandered round
the ward in my bare feet. Next day when the surgeon
visited me I pointed out that my arm was swollen and
inflamed and tried to describe the agonies I was suffering. Now they made an effort to diagnose my complaint
and on 14 September, five weeks after I had left my battalion, the head surgeon operated on my arm. He told
me afterwards that when he drilled the bone, pus simply
shot out of it.

'It had been under very high pressure and must have
caused you terrific pain', he said. It proved that I was
suffering from osteomyelitis, a disease that attacks the
marrow of the bone. I had been operated on for periosti-
tis, a disease which attacks the surface of the bone, when
I was a young lad of about sixteen. My arm still bore
the scars. On that occasion it was thought by the surgeon who performed the operation, Sir Thornley Stoker,
that I should lose my arm, and it was my right arm, but
he managed to save it. The disease broke out again in
subsequent years, once again in my right arm, then in my
left shin bone, then in my left foot and finally in my left

humerus. The last attack occurred in 1928 when I was in India. As I lay in bed in a hospital in Calcutta, I remember hearing the Sister say as she showed the Doctor round the patients, 'You needn't bother about him, he won't last long.' But I had always displayed remarkable powers of recovery, and, having heard that remark, I became more than ever determined that on this occasion, as on the others, I would recover. And I did and the disease never troubled me since, and that was in the year 1928, forty years ago.

The operation in the 42nd General gave me immediate relief and it was not very long before I was up and about again. Leonard also made a good recovery, though his neck was still absolutely stiff and would remain so for many a long day. However, it did not incapacitate him all that much and by the middle of October he was quite game for any fun that was going. And we did have quite a lot of fun. We had been moved about from one hospital to another a good deal and had made friends with quite a few members of the nursing staff.

There were two principal cafés in Salonica; the White Tower Restaurant and the Circle Militaire. The French, who maintained a token force in this war zone, had in their usual fashion made sure that their 'creature comforts' would not be overlooked and they had established the Circle and made sure that it was run in the best possible fashion. Leonard and I used to love to lunch here and to enjoy their vin rouge. Half a litre of it with lunch was enough to give one a very pleasant warm glow. The atmosphere was always gay and the place was generally well filled with French officers and their femmes. They left the dull task of holding the line to the British. There were also some Greek officers to be seen. The Greeks were also supposed to maintain a fighting force, but we never encountered it.

We often entertained our nursing friends at these cafés or arranged picnics with them or even went sailing in the

David Campbell as Captain, wearing MC and the new uniform
sent out from Dublin. His colour badge is Royal Irish Rifles, and
the scroll on the badge says 'Quis Separabit'.

harbour. Sometimes we visited wayside cafés outside the city. They were somewhat primitive but were a bit of fun and a change. We made no attempt at exploring places of historic interest, although Mount Olympus was not so very far away and once we saw it poking a snow-clad head into the sky. Nor did we try to discover traces of St Paul's visits to the city. No doubt we should have read his two epistles to the Thessalonians while we were on the spot. No! We just frittered away our time. But, after all, we were just convalescing and our one idea was just to enjoy our respite from the theatre of war.

My battalion passed through Salonica while I was still detained in hospital there. It was on its way to the Palestine theatre, and my old friend McGavin paid me a short visit. He was not all that keen on the prospect in front of him and told me I was the lucky one in escaping it. I remember little or nothing of the occasion.

On 26 October, a hospital ship was sighted in the harbour and great excitement prevailed amongst all the walking cases. Who would be lucky enough to be evacuated? That was the burning question.

Leonard and I were amongst those warned to be prepared to embark in two days' time and the following day, having lunched at the French Club, we spent the rest of the day bidding adieu to the many nursing friends we had made during our stay. It was not altogether without regret that we parted from them, knowing full well that the likelihood of our ever seeing them again was quite remote.

One or two other reminiscences of Salonica are, perhaps, worthy of mention. I remember a Sunday afternoon in the early days of our occupation, before the villagers had been evacuated, when I went for a ride with my good friends Pollock and McGavin. In one of the villages we visited we encountered what we were told was the ceremony of choosing a bride. All the girls of marriageable age were assembled in the central square.

Here they formed a large circle and, joining hands, they moved around, first in one direction and then in the opposite, beating the ground with their flat, sandalled feet and chanting a monotonous refrain, while the lads of the village stood around in small groups and watched them, at the same time, no doubt, assessing their merits as wives and breadwinners. The girls were dressed in long skirts of party-coloured, coarse-looking material. Some sported a ribbon, others wore a scarf. All of them were broad, stout, hefty-looking wenches. They had need to be, for all the heavy work fell on their shoulders. It was they who did the ploughing and the reaping and the digging. The men were weedy-looking specimens. They just looked on or did the light jobs, and what counted most with them when choosing a wife was brawn, muscle and strength. A modern beauty queen would not have stood an earthly chance of being chosen.

I have watched a family tilling a field. The men sat on a mattress on the headland and kept an eye on the children, and maybe tended a fire on which a meal was cooking, while the mother followed the plough up and down the field. I have seen a family moving along the road, the husband riding a donkey while the wife, with a child on her back and leading another by the hand, padded along behind him.

I noticed the same sort of thing when on a visit to Darjeeling while I was in India. Here, also, women do all the hard work, mend the roads, pick the tea leaves, etc., and are much more strongly built than the men.

The huge buffaloes, used for hauling the night-soil carts, also attracted my attention. I remember meeting a pair of them while so employed one day, a youngster astride one being in control. As they approached me, one of them shook his enormous horns and glared at me through bloodshot eyes. I thought it was going to dash at me and got out of its road pretty quickly. On another occasion I saw one being shod. The shoe smith roped its four legs together and tossed it on its back, its feet sticking up in the air. In such a position he had the buffalo at his mercy and was able to get on with the shoeing.

When describing the mode of travel of a peasant family in Macedonia, with the father mounted on a donkey, leading, and the mother and children on foot trailing behind, I forgot to mention that nowadays, as I am told, where similar modes of progress are adopted, as in Saigon or Nigeria, the mother and children take the lead, just in case of landmines.

10

Hospital Ship to England

29 October 1917

We sailed from Salonica on the hospital ship *Formosa* on 29 October, eleven weeks after I had left my battalion. I don't think we had any idea where we were bound for, but in four or five days we found ourselves in Valetta harbour. We disembarked on the day after our arrival, Leonard and I and the other surgical cases being sent to Tighni Hospital and the medical cases to St Andrew's Hospital.

Nothing was done to my arm while we were in Malta, except that it was dressed three or four times a week. I had discarded my sling several weeks before and did not feel incommoded at all. Leonard, although his neck was still as stiff as ever, was not otherwise incapacitated and was likewise ready to take part in any activity that offered distraction or entertainment, and we did have plenty of both during our four-week stay there.

The hospital was very comfortable and few restrictions were placed on our activities. Walking cases like Leonard and I could, to all intents and purposes, do as we pleased, so long as we kept to certain hours. There was, however, one important restriction placed on our activities, to wit, we were forbidden to have drinks in public bars, and to distinguish us from others to whom the restriction did not apply, we had to wear blue armbands. Drinks could, however, be served to us with meals, in hotels and at the Union Club.

A first-class Italian Opera company, marooned in Malta for the duration of the war, gave frequent performances at the Opera House. Leonard and I promptly reserved a box there. We also joined the Union Club, which was open to officers of the Army and the Navy.

I remember our first visit to the Opera. We were accompanied by two nursing friends. Our box was near the stage and we had a splendid view of the auditorium. It was shaped like a horse shoe; the stage being at the open end and the Governor's box at the tip of the shoe. There were no galleries. Tiers of boxes rose from the floor to the ceiling. Rows of seats filled the floor space, the pit. My impression was that the boxes were occupied by the British and the pit by the Maltese. The opera on this occasion was *Tosca*. We could not understand the words, of course, as it was sung in Italian, but, very likely, there was a description in English which gave us some idea of what it was all about. At any rate we enjoyed it very much. I thought the voices were wonderful and that I had never before heard anything like them. The acting, too, was marvellous; so demonstrative, so full of gesture, so eloquent in expression. One did not need to know the words. (Can one ever catch them, anyhow, even in one's own language?)

The response by the Maltese in the pit was worth seeing. From where we sat we could see their faces. What a reception they gave the show! Aware of every nuance, they responded to all the finer points made by the actors, and their applause must have been a tonic to the latter. It made me feel the complete philistine, quite lacking in the culture presumed needful for the full appreciation of the show I was watching.

Dinner at the Union Club and a box at the opera a couple of times a week became an established routine during our stay. It was our way of entertaining our friends.

Looking around the boxes, we were able to recognise quite a few people we knew and during the intervals we either visited them or received visits. It was all great fun and we felt we were enjoying the high life in very earnest.

The climate of Malta is of course very delightful in November and we took advantage of it by going for drives into the country. There were no taxis in those days but we found the horse-drawn cabs comfortable and not too slow. The surface is a succession of hills and valleys and is terraced everywhere and divided into small fields. I remember being amused at the sizes of the fields. They were so tiny in comparison with the broad acres to which I was accustomed in my native Co. Louth. Intensive cultivation was practised, apparently. We visited many places of interest and some of the seaside resorts. We also visited St Paul's Cathedral and saw the original Maltese Cross.

The British community in Valetta was well organised and made a point of entertaining the inmates of the military hospitals and so we often found ourselves attending tennis at-homes, and concerts and dances. The Governor of Malta, Lord Methuen, also felt it was his duty to take some notice of those who were in uniform and entertained batches of us from time to time. I was present at one of his at-homes and later was a guest at a luncheon at the Palace. This was considered quite a distinction for me as not everyone in uniform was so honoured. Those who made out the list of guests had to be careful to exclude everyone suspected of being a malingerer, or of 'swinging the lead', as we say, and there were quite a few of those in Valetta. The fact that I wore the ribbon of the MC and a wound stripe saved me from being regarded as one of them.

At the luncheon, I was placed next to the Governor's daughter, a young lady in her early twenties, I should say. On the whole, I think I felt rather embarrassed. While listening to the lady's chatter, I put down my knife and fork a couple of times and then had to hurry to catch up. I am afraid she must have found me dull company. She appeared to be somewhat highbrow; played the violin, ran concerts, ran an orchestra and that sort of thing. No doubt she soon discovered I had no accomplishments she could make use of, and so we parted without making any commitments except that I promised to go to a concert she was giving next day.

As for the rest, Leonard and I often enjoyed a game of snooker or billiards either at the Union Club or at the hospital. He had the edge on me at snooker though I was able to hold my own at billiards, generally. I well remember our last game of billiards. It was on the day of our departure from Malta. We had gone aboard the hospital ship *Wandilla* in the afternoon, having duly celebrated the event around the city. We had shed our blue armbands at the hospital and were free to buy drinks wherever we liked, and we liked a good many places. After dinner aboard ship we heard that the sailing was postponed till the next day and one and all applied for shore leave, which the captain granted, up till midnight (very foolishly, I think). So ashore we went and celebrated our departure for the second time.

During the course of the evening, Leonard and I and some half-dozen others found ourselves at the Union Club. It was then that the challenge match between Leonard and me took place. Well, the game progressed and Leonard at 95 led me by 15. It looked as if it were all over. Several of our friends who were watching had bets on the match. My bet with Leonard was a pound. We had been celebrating pretty freely since we came ashore and I was none too steady on my feet and had to cling to the cushion as I moved around the table. Nevertheless, when I got in at 80, I kept on scoring, each shot being greeted with applause, much to the annoyance of those playing at the other tables who had not been celebrating as we had, and who cast disapproving looks in our direction, and, believe it or not, I reached the 100 with my 20 break unfinished and won the match. I had great pleasure in collecting my pound from my good friend who had so often collected half a crown from me at our various other encounters. That was the event of the evening, though we afterwards fell in with some naval officers who insisted on us coming to their club where dancing was in progress, and insisted on standing us some more drinks.

That was the last we saw of Malta. We had a very pleasant four-week stay there and had made many friends. On the whole I think we heaved a sigh of regret as we left it all behind.

We encountered rather stormy weather on the voyage home and many were sick. I, however, escaped that fate. The trip was without incident, though we were kept on the *qui vive* by frequent warnings of the presence of submarines in our vicinity. At Bristol, where we landed, we were told we had been lucky as the hospital ship that preceded us had been torpedoed, and also the one that followed us. We had indeed been more than lucky. On disembarking, I was sent to the 3rd London General Hospital at Clapham Junction. I never discovered where Leonard was, nor did I ever hear of him again.

11

Back in England

29 October 1917

My stay in the 3rd London was on the whole a pleasant enough experience. I soon made friends with other walking cases in my ward and together we set out to explore and sample the amenities, amusements, pleasures and entertainments on offer in the city. I am afraid we gave a wide berth to places of interest such as museums, art galleries and the like. It was the more frivolous amenities that drew us.

I however made a pilgrimage to Westminster Abbey and to St Paul's Cathedral. In St Paul's I stood before the statue of General James Wolfe and recalled how, as he sailed down the St Lawrence towards Quebec, he read Gray's 'Elegy' to the officers with him in the boat. When he read the line, 'The paths of glory lead but to the grave', he paused and said, 'I'd rather have been the author of that line than to take Quebec tomorrow.'

The words proved to have been prophetic, for in the hour of victory, after being thrice wounded, he died on the battlefield, but not before he had been assured by his officers that the French had been completely routed. 'I die contented', were his last words. I remember now that as a youth I regarded General Wolfe as my hero, and that I could not hold back my tears when I first gazed upon his statue.

But, as I have said, it was the lighter side of London life that attracted us; the theatres, restaurants, saloons, dives, etc. We visited as many as we could fit in. Scarcely a day passed that we did not visit some show or dine at some well-known hotel or restaurant, or wine at some famous saloon. It was indeed an extravagant, foolish sort of life we led.

Although we saw a good many shows, only two linger in my memory; *Choo Chin Chow* and *The Thirteenth Chair*, in which Mrs Patrick Campbell took the lead. I can still feel the ghostly terror aroused by the latter and I still love to recall the magnificence and the haunting melodies of the former. Many a time and oft I have found myself humming 'I sit and cobble'. I also remember a song I first heard at the Trocadero when having tea there on an occasion. It was 'Roses are blooming in Picardy'. No doubt I have heard it since but I only remember that first occasion.

Few restrictions were placed on our movements. We had to be at our bedsides, of course, when the MO was making his rounds and we had to be in by 10p.m. Even the latter restriction was taken off if an air raid happened to be on. That meant that if you were caught in town you could stay put till the raid was over. Air raids were not frequent or terrifying. They did serve to remind us however that there was still a war on. Perhaps our feverish pleasure-seeking was attributable to a desire to forget this and to forget that the respite we were enjoying was only a temporary one. One of these days we should have to return to the battlefield again.

My arm was not troubling me much at this time but the wound refused to heal. A couple of weeks after my arrival at the hospital, however, they put me on the operating table and scraped out the wound and six weeks later, on 13 February 1918, I was discharged from hospital.

Shortly after I reached London, I paid a visit to Cox & Co. and found that, in spite of my extravagant way of living since leaving the battalion, I had still a credit balance of £370. Thereupon, I made my first investment by putting £250 into War Bonds. When checking my account, I found that the six golden sovereigns I had drawn from the Field Cashier at Mudros had not been debited to my account. I had arrived at Highclere Castle two years previously with all six intact, but before I had left there they had been transmuted into paper money while I made my first attempts at playing Poker, Pontoon, Slippery Sam, Chemin-de-fer, Rouge-et-Noir and Contract Bridge; all except one had gone. I used it to tip the butler as I left the castle. I haven't seen a sovereign since.

I did not completely forget my good friend Lady Carnarvon who had nursed me on my return from Gallipoli. By now she had transferred her hospital from Highclere Castle to her house in Bryanston Square. She gave me a terrific welcome when I called on her there. Taking my arm, she led me round the various rooms where the patients were accommodated and proudly showed me to them. She was so delighted I had been made a Captain and awarded the MC. A week later she had me in to lunch and again made no end of a fuss about me and tried to make me feel proud of myself. It is one of my greatest regrets that I never afterwards made an attempt to get in touch with her and express my gratitude for all she had done for me.

Towards the end of the winter, I made inquiries about having my MC conferred and was told to write to the Lord Chamberlain on the subject. This I did and in the course of a few days I received a letter from him telling me to present myself at Buckingham Palace for the Investiture due to take place on a certain date. There was nobody I could ask to accompany me, so all alone and unsupported I set out from the hospital. My train from Clapham Junction brought me as far as Charing Cross and from there to the Palace I took a taxi. A blizzard was raging at the time and there were great heaps of half-melted snow and slush along the footpath. Into the middle of one of these monstrous heaps I stepped from the taxi. Halfway up to my knees it came, making a horrible mess of my boots and leggings. How I ever got myself cleaned up and made presentable I do not remember but I do remember how terribly upset I was and how worried lest I should be late for my appointment.

In the Picture Gallery of the Palace, where we assembled, I found myself one of a gathering of about fifty, and there we were put through the drill and told what to do:

> On your name being called you will advance smartly to the throne on which the King will be seated. Halt, turn to your left and take three steps forward. You will then hold out your left hand to the King. He will take your hand in his left, say a few words to you and fix your medal on the hook already fixed to your tunic. You will then take three steps backwards and return to your place.

(The King, George V, had broken his right arm in a hunting accident a short time previously and so he had to use his left hand to make the presentations.)

It was marvellous what a feeling of loyalty surged through my breast as he clasped my hand and thanked me for my services. My wildest youthful dreams never included having my hand grasped by the King. My sister Mollie, her husband Glover and my niece Marion have also had the honour of being presented to royalty. Each was awarded the MBE.

The round of frivolities continued over Christmas and the New Year and I even made a flying visit to Dublin, though I did not visit Crinstown on that occasion. Although this was one of the blackest periods of the war, it made no great impression on me at the time. When I went to Waterloo Station to see off a friend who was returning to France after recovering from wounds, I felt to the full the impact of the situation. The platforms were packed with a seething mass of humanity. Here was a young soldier in full kit and trailing a kitbag behind him and with his rifle slung on his shoulder, and was that his wife who clung to him, or his sister, or his fiancée? And there was a mother and three or four children come to see Daddy off and fully aware that they might never see him again. A group of youngsters in fresh new uniforms and making their first visit to the front kept up their spirits with the lively refrain:

Bon soir, old thing,
Cheerio, chinchin.
Nopoo, Toodleoo,
Goodbye.

And a young officer 'With a smile on his lips
And his Lieutenant's pips,
Upon his shoulder, bright and gay.'

What a medley of tears and sighs and brave smiles. And as the train pulled out, there were some who had to be dragged away from the carriage windows. It was all so tragic, so sad, so heart wrenching, all this sacrifice of human life. And my own turn might come again in the not so very distant future.

At long last, after nine weeks in the 3rd London General and six months after I had left our front line in Salonica, I was boarded and found fit to proceed on leave. That was on 13 February 1918.

I was given three weeks leave and immediately headed for home. I spent the first week or so showing myself to various relations in Co. Kildare and visiting friends in New Ross and Dublin. The rest of my leave I spent at Crinstown. I played golf nearly every day at Ardee or Dundalk and felt myself getting stronger every day. But 'Golden minutes swiftly run, Passing e'er they've yet begun', and before I realised it my leave had expired and I was on my way back to report for duty. It was 13 March 1918.

On this occasion I was posted to the 3rd Royal Irish Rifles in Belfast. I thought of how nervous I was when I reported to the 4th Battalion on 4 January 1916. I had travelled about a bit since then and it was without fear or trepidation that I now presented myself.

I was placed in command of 'D' Company and I presume I carried out the ordinary duties of a Company Commander. I remember very little of that side of the life. What I do remember, though, is that the principal function of the battalion was to re-equip and dispatch officers and men to the battalions of the Rifles then serving in France. Most of these drafts had already seen service and were now being sent back to their units.

It was a time of great anxiety. The Great German Offensive had opened and our troops were falling back on all fronts. Casualties were very heavy. Many prisoners were being taken. The prospect in front of the drafts was indeed a dismal one.

At this time I remember sitting down to a game of Pontoon one evening in the Mess with eight or nine others. Six of them were due to leave for France in the morning. They were having their last fling, or perhaps endeavouring to put out of their minds the ordeal, indeed the dreadful ordeal that lay in front of them. The game was hectic. Rounds of drinks followed every Pontoon. The stakes were high, at least for young officers. It was all very exciting, but when the game ended at midnight they had to bid their goodbyes and steel their hearts once more to the grim prospects ahead. And so it went on from week to week. Whose turn would it be next? How could we help being anxious?

But all was not gloom all the time. A group of young officers and their civilian friends formed themselves into a sort of entertainments committee and organised dances and concerts and theatre parties and various other forms of interest and amusement. I remember on one occasion being inveigled into playing goalkeeper in a mixed hockey match. I had never played hockey before. That, I was told, didn't matter. All I had to do was to keep the ball from getting into the net. I agreed to do my best to achieve this aim. All went well and I stopped the ball on several occasions, once too often, perhaps, as will be seen later on. I was wearing my ordinary boots and leather leggings as I stopped the ball with my left foot, the one which had been wounded in Gallipoli. It did not hurt me much at the time, but as I have just said, more about this later on.

On another occasion I was one of a theatre party. Half a dozen of us occupied a box near the stage. We had just dined and wined, and were no doubt feeling a bit uppish. A girl in a blue, white-spotted frock sang 'Sprinkle me with kisses', and some of us rolled up bits of paper and flicked them towards her. Maybe we joined in the chorus and were generally noisy and obstreperous. At any rate, during the course of the evening the APM knocked at the door of our box and warned us to behave ourselves. He did not take any of our names.

A few days later I found myself on the mat before the GOC. The APM had sent my description to our CO, reporting that I was the senior officer in a noisy party at the theatre. The description fitted several others. I was the least suspected and was only discovered after the others had supplied alibis. The description was that of a Captain wearing the ribbon of the Military Cross. It fitted one whom I afterwards knew in Dublin as an eye specialist. I, of course had to admit I was guilty when I appeared before the CO. He sent me to the GOC. It was the first time I had ever been 'on the mat' and I was badly frightened. I am like that. The General gave me a nice little lecture and made me feel very sorry for myself. I swore I would never do such a thing again. I was not allowed to forget the incident for quite some time, especially by those who had been questioned but were able to prove an alibi.

The dances made little impression on me and though I met a good many of my colleagues' sisters, etc., I formed no attachments.

Our afternoons must have been fairly free from duties and I see from my diary that I was able to play golf three or four times a week. Bangor was our favourite venue but we also patronised Malone occasionally.

Amidst all these attractions and distractions, all these comings and goings, the time passed pleasantly enough and we were able to keep at bay thoughts or worries about what was happening in the war zones.

A note instructing me to appear before a Medical Board on 16 April jolted me back to a full consciousness of the realities of the situation. Would I be passed fit and sent out to hazard my life once again? It was not to be just yet. I was given a month's Home Service. A short reprieve, but still a reprieve. And I was glad, for had I been passed fit and sent out to the trenches in France I should, at that time, have stood a very small chance of survival.

A week or two later, the battalion moved over to Durrington Camp on Salisbury Plain and arrived quite unheralded apparently. On the march from the railway station I went lame in my left foot and when, on arriving at the camp, I removed my boot, the foot was swollen and inflamed where the hockey ball had hit it during that goalkeeping episode in Belfast. I sometimes regard the latter episode as an act of Providence for had it not occurred I might well have been pushing up the poppies 'In Flanders Fields', where they 'blow between the crosses, row on row', that mark the places of the dead. Perhaps, I sometimes thought, I was being preserved for another destiny – to be the happy father and proud grandfather of worthy descendants.

In a couple of days' time I was admitted to Fargo Hospital and, on my foot being x-rayed, the trouble was diagnosed as osteomyelitis (inflammation of the bone marrow) of the first metatarsal (the bone next to the joint of the big toe). My old bone disease had attacked again. On the last occasion it was my right arm that had suffered. My foot was operated on in due course and the dead bone cut out. Then, while I was still in Fargo, I received a letter from the War Office, dated 1 June 1918, informing me that as I had exhausted all the sick leave to which I was entitled, there was no alternative but to have me gazetted as having relinquished my Commission owing to ill health. I would be granted the honorary rank of Captain and my case would be referred to the Ministry of Pensions for any claims as to retired pay or disability allowance. The notice of my retirement appeared in the *Gazette* of 14 June 1918.

So my career in the Army ended, somewhat ignominiously, it appears to me now. At the time I was somewhat dazed by the turn of events but I don't think I was all that displeased at escaping the risk of having to join my comrades in the trenches ever again.

12

Epilogue: I am retired

1 June 1918

Perhaps this would be a suitable place to refer to my Military Cross and Mention in Despatches. To my queries on the subject I received the following replies from the War Office:

Ministry of Defence
4 December 1968

Sir,

I am directed to reply to your letter dated 12 November 1968, regarding a citation for your award of the Military Cross. The award was published in the *London Gazette* dated 4 June 1917.
 As this was an Honours Gazette, no citations are available.

Signed,
Military Secretary

'Preamble' to the *London Gazette* dated 21 July 1917

General Headquarters
Salonica

29 March 1917

My Lord,

I have the honour to submit a list of names of the Officers, Warrant Officers, etc., whose services I wish to bring to your notice for distinguished service rendered during the past six months in this theatre of operations.

Signed,
G.F. Milne
Lieutenant-General

Included in the list of names is that of Temp. Lt (Temp. Capt.) D. Campbell, Royal Irish Rifles.

An account of my life during the months that followed can only come as an anticlimax. It was a case of being passed on from one hospital to another with a couple of short intervals at home, while all the time there rankled at the back of my mind a vague uneasiness regarding my future.

My last call was at the Richmond Hospital, Dublin, which I reached on 28 October 1918, six months after I had left Fargo Hospital on Salisbury Plain. Here I had two further operations on my foot and spent five months on my back in bed, being finally discharged towards the end of March 1919.

I had escaped the great flu epidemic of 1918, although it had been rampant in the Richmond and scarce a day passed that we did not see one or more patients moved up to the 'Death Ward' whence none ever returned. I had joined in the first Armistice Day (11 November 1918) celebrations with a glass of insipid white wine, and I had been taught how to play Cribbage by a Canadian Officer who used to collect quite a few of my pennies.

As I headed for home after this, the dreariest period of my life, I should have been bright and gay. But I wasn't.

Indeed I shall never forget my first walk down the fields a few days after my arrival. My knees were knocking together. I looked a miserable specimen, for all the world like a calf with scour. You wouldn't have given two pence for my chances of survival. Indeed we all thought my days were numbered, and I laugh now on this, my eighty-second birthday, when I find that that was fifty-one years ago and that I am still hale and hearty and can, and often do, boast of my no fewer than nine grandchildren, all sturdy, and healthy children, and I thank God a thousand times.

Nothing forgotten when they were begotten,
Nothing left out when they came about.

13

Rehabilitation

1 June 1918

I was not very long at home when I began to recover my health. The air of my native heath and the simple food to which I was accustomed in my youth soon began to tell and ere ever the summer was far spent I was sitting up and taking notice again.

The prospect in front of me was a grim one. As Tennyson, in 'Locksley Hall', puts it:

What is that which I should turn to,
Lighting upon days like these?
Every door is barr'd with gold
And opens but to golden keys.

Every gate is throng'd with suitors,
all the markets overflow.
I have but an angry fancy,
what is that which I should do?

I had no profession, no qualification, no trade or business experience. Thousands upon thousands of others were in like straits. They had just been demobbed and thrown on the labour market. Some tried to eke out a miserable existence by selling matches or picture postcards on the streets. There never had been so many unemployed nor ever so few vacancies.

Like everyone else I was at a loss to know what to do. I made one or two feeble attempts at getting a job. Trinity College was offering free courses of various kinds. Motor engineering was one of these and I thought I would join it. I found it was being conducted in a technical school at Ringsend.

I took up my abode at Hotel Gerard in Harcourt Street and began attending the classes. As soon as I arrived I was given a file and put to work at a bench. My job was to reduce two pieces of flat steel to the same size and rivet them together. As soon as I began to work the instructor drew the attention of the whole class to the way I handled my file. 'Here's a man who knows how to use his hands', he said, or words to that effect. There were about ten in the class, one of whom stayed at my hotel. Some of them had progressed to using lathes and other power-driven tools. Between times we were given lectures on the motor engine and lessons in driving a car. I worked away at my two pieces of steel for perhaps three weeks but when I came to rivet them together they did not match all that well. I was in despair. Then my foot gave in again. All this standing at the bench proved too much for it. It was then I entered the Richmond Hospital as already described. So ended my attempt at becoming a motor engineer.

After I was discharged from hospital some six months later and had somewhat recovered my health, a further three months later, I made another attempt at getting work. This time I applied for a job as secretary to a branch of the Farmers' Union, which I saw advertised. There were other candidates also present and I was not the one selected, thank Heaven. Then I thought I would join a cinema film distributing agency which was being started by two men who wanted a third partner who would be prepared to put some capital into the business. I agreed to give the proposal two weeks trial. In the first week I travelled round the country with them while they visited cinemas and offered their films for hire. In the second week I travelled round by myself. I was not at all happy in the work. I was too shy to become friendly with other travellers I met on the trains and in the hotels and had little confidence in my ability to impress the cinema managers. I decided the job was not in my line and that I would hold on to my little capital for another while.

14

Return to Trinity College

1 September 1919

It was then that I learnt that the government was giving grants to officers who wished to complete their University education which had been interrupted by their service with the Forces. I applied for and was given a grant, which would enable me to take out a Degree in Civil Engineering in Trinity College Dublin. Away back in 1914, I had been studying with a view to entering the ministry of the Church of Ireland, but by now my views on the subject had changed and I had come to the conclusion that Engineering would be more in my line than Divinity.

And now a different life began. I had to become a student again. Away back in 1914, a full five years previously, I had kicked my Greek lexicon in the air, symbolising my delight at being free from the need to continue studying, and had gladly put my other books away. I did not consider whether I should ever have to open them again. The problem was too remote. Now, at the age of thirty-two, I should have to take out my textbooks again and resume my studies where I had left off. Did I say, 'where I had left off'? What a hope! When I opened my trigonometry book, I found I had to begin at page one. I had forgotten what a cosine was. As for logarithms, all knowledge of them had faded from my mind. And so it was with most of the other subjects. Fortunately, I had not to take up Greek or Latin again. So to begin with, it was a very hard struggle indeed. And, before I could avail of my grant, I had to pass the entrance examination to the Engineering School, then only three months away.

> If you can force your heart and nerve and sinew
> To serve your turn, long after they are gone

Yes! That describes what I had to do. But my goodness, it was a hard struggle. However, by hook or by crook, I managed to pass the exam, thank Heaven. Perhaps the examiners were a bit lenient on fellows like me.

As I packed my trunk and headed for Dublin, I felt I was setting out on a fresh adventure, that I was on the threshold of a new career and my spirit leapt within me at the prospect. I knew not what lay ahead but I allowed my ambition to soar; I indulged in the wildest of dreams, the greatest of expectations.

On reaching Dublin, I installed myself at 91 Ranelagh Road, where I shared digs with one Fred Little, who afterwards became my close friend, and a Dr Dunlop who was working for his Fellowship (FRCSI) and we made a happy trio. I remember little of the day-to-day routine of the college. One thing, however, sticks in my memory and has troubled me ever since. It was my start in the drawing class. To begin with the class was set to draw a plummer block, plan elevation, section. But first we had to print the title. How I laboured at that printing. How I sweated over it; sweated blood, if that were possible. I spent days and days at it, but still it was a poor result. I was in despair. I was afraid I should never succeed and was contemplating throwing in the sponge when I saw another attempt even worse than mine. So I carried on. My attempts at drawing the plummer block were equally futile and eventually

I just copied my neighbours. I am sure I spent a couple of weeks over this, my first attempt at making a drawing, weeks of despair and frustration. Then we went on to drawing projections and shadows and again I was baffled and had to be helped out by one of my classmates. Indeed I never fully mastered this subject.

However in the long run, taking days over tasks others completed in hours, I began to make a little headway. But I never became a skilful draughtsman, a handicap I felt throughout the rest of my career. One of the lecturers used to console me by telling me that it didn't always pay to become too good a draughtsman as you might be doomed to spend the rest of your life bending over a drawing board or miss promotion or transfer to a better post because you could not be spared from the drawing office. I've known such a thing to happen. In any case my inclination lay in the direction of the execution rather than the design of works.

Some of the subjects –, chemistry, mineralogy, palae-ontology and geology – I took to readily enough. Indeed the last one, geology, actually aroused my enthusiasm. The lecturer on this subject, Dr Joly, was himself an enthusiast, and a world figure in this subject and in astronomy. He, it will be remembered, had a hand in the invention and development of colour photography. He had the power, too, of transmitting his enthusiasm to his pupils. My interest in geology still survives and I still love to open again my textbook on the subject.

I met Dr Joly once in later life. It was in the early summer of 1927, when I was home on leave from India. There was a total eclipse of the sun visible from Conway in North Wales, which I thought I should like to see. On the way over on the boat to Holyhead I spotted my much-admired Joly amongst the passengers. He was all dressed up in frock coat and tall silk hat; suitable attire for the great occasion, and for the attendance at the conference of astronomers, assembled there from many parts of the world. I can still picture the weird silence that developed on the seafront as the eclipse became total. And maybe I noted the birds going to roost in the trees, thinking it was night, or maybe I just read that in a book. Another thing that struck me was the large number of youths on motorbikes chasing up and down the promenade, the cynosure of the eyes of an equally large number of maidens doing ditto on foot.

Other subjects I took to readily were applied mechanics and mathematical physics. The theory of electricity and the differential calculus were a bit beyond my comprehension. I took in enough of them with the textbooks at my elbow.

I thought I should like to give a picture of my life in college during those three and a half years but I now find it is a bit outside my capability. I shall therefore content myself with describing a few of the highlights.

It was in October 1919 that I returned to Trinity, having passed the entrance examination to the Engineering School. As I said at the beginning of my narrative, I was preparing to sit 'Little Go' when the war broke out in 1914. I was afraid I should have to take that examination on my return and I had a feeling that I should not be able to manage it. It was a terrific relief, therefore, when I found I would be allowed it. I kept my Arts, Jun. Soph. year by lectures, likewise my Sen. Soph. year 1920. Then in December of that year I sat for my BA degree exam.

More than three quarters of the men in my class were ex-servicemen and nearly all of us had joined the OTC. It gave us an opportunity of getting to know one another. This was a pleasant exercise, but it had its dangers. It led to too much waste of time, too many meetings at various haunts around the city and sometimes too many drinks. It would have been better if we had spent (as the sensible ones had) more time over our books and less time spending our grants and amusing ourselves.

The first Remembrance Day Dinner was held in the Dining Hall on 11 November 1919. Our class was present in full strength. Eight of us met in Jammet's before hand and had sherries. Someone remarked that we were already

'lit up' even before the dinner began. It was on this occasion that Major Harris, the chairman, said in his speech,
as I have already related, 'And here is Sergeant Campbell,
discharged as "inefficient" in August 1914 and given a
commission and comes back a Captain with his breast
covered with ribbons.' That was what one might call a
hilarious dinner.

I was made a Sergeant as soon as I joined the OTC
and a year later was made Sgt Major of the Engineering
Company. This gave me a prominent position in the
Engineering School, a position I should not have attained
by my academic achievements alone. And to this day (1970)
when I meet any of them, my former NCOs are inclined
to click their heels when they address me.

During this year, 1919, and the greater part of 1920,
I worked pretty hard, yet I wasted a lot of time gadding
around, going to dances and parties of various kinds. And
as well as attending to my work in the Engineering School
I had also to prepare for my BA exam, now only a couple
of months away. At this point Fate stepped in and took a
hand in my affairs.

As I was cycling in to college one wet morning, my bike
skidded on a tram rail and down I came on my right side
with the hell of a bump. I picked myself up and continued
my journey. Then, when halfway through the first lecture,
and having some difficulty in guiding my pen, I reached
over with my left hand to feel my right elbow and there
I found a lump as big as an egg. By now, too, the pain had
become more intense and the effects of the shock had begun
to tell. I attended no more lectures that day (nor indeed for
many a long day afterwards). Indeed it was all I could do to
get back to my digs.

Dr Dunlop arranged for my admission to the Adelaide
Hospital and on being x-rayed a Y-shaped fracture into
the elbow joint was revealed. Mr Gunn, the surgeon who
took charge of my case, describing it to his class, called it
a green-tree fracture and expressed the opinion that I was

likely to be left with a stiff elbow. He was wrong, thank Heaven.

It might be thought that the accident would have ruined my chances of getting my exam. The effect, however, was the opposite. It pulled me up, halted me in my stride, compelled me to quit gadding around and wasting my time, and left me with no alternative but to get on with my studies. I have often thought that but for this interference of Fate, these six weeks of compulsory immobility, I might have failed my exam. As it turned out, I had barely time to cover the ground. With three days to go I tackled my last book, *Young's Astronomy*. It was a description of the planets and took my fancy. Once I took it up I became totally absorbed in it and never left it down till I had finished it, though it took me a day and half a night.

It was while I was in hospital that I first met my future wife, Ruth Flavelle. She was the medical student in charge of my case, and I remember how she used to visit me every morning, look at my chart and inquire how I was getting on. We met again at the BA exam, and I have an idea I was able to give her some tips about the astronomy viva. Thus it turned out that my fall off my bicycle proved to be providential in more ways than one.

I had one close call in the vivas. It was in mathematical physics. My examiner, Harry Thrift, spent at least a quarter of an hour trying to discover something I knew of the subject, but without success. I had a complete blackout; couldn't remember a thing. However, I had been a member of his class, indeed one of the brightest members, and frequently answered questions he put to the class. He remembered this now and gave me a pass mark saying, 'I know you know the subject and I'll let you through.' It was an anxious moment for me. I was afraid he might give me a duck. Some of my mates said that he did not fail me because I was wearing the ex-servicemen's badge and had my arm in a sling.

My arm was still very painful and I could not write with

David Campbell in OTC uniform. He was made Sgt Major of the Engineering Company.

my usual speed or legibility. I was greatly relieved therefore when I found I had passed. I felt quite a different person when I had the degree BA conferred on me. That was one obstacle surmounted. Now I could devote all my time and energy to my work in the Engineering School and prepare for the final obstacle, the BAI degree examination in October 1922, nearly two years away.

In 1921 I really did get down to work. I remember how I used to peel off my coat, seize myself by the hair and force myself into the chair at my work table. Then I used to practice Couéism, and, by repeating time and again, 'Hard work is really enjoyable', I almost convinced myself that it was so. I did stick to my studies that year.

Nevertheless, I found time to attend a five-day course in musketry at Hythe, in Kent, that year, organised by the OTC, an uncalled-for and foolish relapse, I agree. I also found time to attend a two-week camp at Conway with the OTC. My position as CSM of the Engineering Unit gave me some excuse for this.

While we were in camp the results of the term exam in Maths and Physics were posted on the noticeboard, and when he heard of this one of my sergeants, Hamilton by name, called out, 'Come along, lads and let's see who were the poor devils that failed.' What a sell he got when his own name was the first he saw among the failures. And he had organised a party of some ten of his class whom he had coached. I was pleased when I found I had got through with good marks.

I took Certificates A and B in 1921 in the OTC and, in recognition of the latter, was presented with their highest award for efficiency, a Malacca cane with a beautifully embossed silver knob. Sad to relate the embossed knob came to a tragic end when it got bashed in during a 'Rag' that followed a win in the final of the 'Cup' by the rugby team. I had it replaced by a plain knob, but the substitution did not escape the notice of my friend, Miss Ruth Flavelle.

This was the year we held the Ball in the Gresham, the

first of its kind held by the Engineers. I was the Hon. Sec.; indeed it was I got it up. It turned out to be a great success, but it was many a long day before another such dance was held outside College. 'The Troubles', the Civil War, the Black and Tans intervened and put an end to such frivolities.

Strange to say, 'The Troubles' made very little impression on our minds and I remember very little about them. True, the rattle of musketry at night sometimes disturbed my slumbers, and the curfew, when imposed, caused me a certain amount of inconvenience. I remember an occasion when attending a dance in the Café Cairo in Grafton Street, when we had to be there before the curfew began at 10p.m. and couldn't leave till it terminated at 6a.m. On another occasion, when returning from a dance with my two pals Fred Little and Bill Harkness, we were stopped by three drunk Black and Tans in Wicklow Street. Harkness had the wit to fade away but Little would argue with them. They waved their guns in front of our faces and abused us, calling us the dirtiest names under the sun, while each moment we expected the guns to go off. Finally, after kicking out at us, they drove us off. We still had the three miles back to our digs and were fearful of other hold-ups, but managed to reach them in safety. That was my worst fright during this period.

I really knew very little of what was going on. I didn't take a daily paper – had no time for such reading – and there was no radio or television in those days to strike terror into our souls. How different to the 'Troubles' in Belfast and Londonderry in 1969, when every event, of however little significance, was seized upon by all three news media – press, radio and television – and dinned into our ears and emblazoned before our eyes, until we were sick, sore and tired of the whole business.

We lost one of our year, a close friend of mine, during the troubled times. His people were big landowners in Co. Cork, and, like many another Protestant landowner, were wiped out to the last man and their homes burned to the ground.

In general, during those times, Trinity was, as far as I could see, left undisturbed and went her own sweet way, apparently oblivious to what was happening outside her walls.

Now I come to my last year in Trinity, 1922. It was a year of concentrated toil. Never in all my life have I worked so hard. And I received my due reward, for, when the result of the final examination was published, I found I had scored 78 per cent, a First Class Honour mark, and had come out third top in my class. The class was a record one of eighty students, the highest ever, and the two students who had scored higher marks than I were both scholars, and were young men whose studies had not been interrupted by war service. I was thirty-five years old at the time and I reckon this was a fine achievement, one of my best, and I have always been proud of it.

As soon as the exams were over, I went in to the Adelaide for an operation on my right arm. An abscess had been growing for some weeks and at the time I feared I should have to give up my work. It was the old trouble, osteomyelitis. They cut open the bone and scraped it out and I was in circulation again in five or six weeks' time.

On my first day out, I paid a visit to Miss Flavelle, who in the meantime had taken her MB and BCH and was doing a locum at Blessington, while she prepared to take her DPH. The journey on the top of the old steam tram was not the acme of comfort. There were deep drifts of beech leaves on the side of the road in Blessington, through which I waded with glee.

And now I had to find myself a job; not an easy task in those days with so many applicants in the field and so few vacancies. I seized upon the first opportunity that offered itself. One of my year, Phillips by name, had obtained a job as assistant to the Resident Engineer on a dock and harbour construction project at Workington, Cumberland and through his mediation his contractors took me on as unpaid assistant. I accepted the offer for the purpose of gaining experience and because I felt that I would stand a better chance of getting a worthwhile appointment if I was already in employment.

Working for nothing is not a very attractive business. Nevertheless I enjoyed my stay in Workington. I had my small pension from the Ministry of Pensions and after about six months the contractors gave me a pound a week. I was able to join the golf club and had not as dull a time as might be expected. Then my pension was stopped. This was a bad blow and my spirit sank into my shoes. By the end of the year, I had almost reached the end of my resources.

I appealed against the decision of the Medical Board, which had stopped my pension, and was sent to London for a retrial of my case. This was quite an amusing encounter. All three members of the Board were Irishmen and all three were graduates of Trinity, and most of the questions I was asked were about various members of the Trinity staff. I did succeed in impressing upon them, however, that my main reason for seeking the restoration of my pension was that I should be able to claim my hospital expenses whenever I had to lay up for repairs, which happened every two or three years. They were very decent and granted me a disability allowance of 20 per cent, the minimum appropriate to my rank, for life. It then amounted to only £42 a year, but I was jolly glad of it. Later I was allowed wife and children allowances and increases were granted from time to time, and my hospital expenses were paid on a good number of occasions. Today it amounts to £117, and, being free of tax, is worth half as much again and is still highly appreciated, and I haven't had to lie up for repairs for forty years now and my percentage disability is just nil in so far as it is affected by the old osteomyelitis.

Before the results of my appeal came through and when I had been about a year in Workington, news of vacancies for engineers with experience in harbour construction reached us. The advertisers were the Calcutta

Port Commissioners and the project was a £25 million one. The news caused quite a stir but Phillips and I were the only ones in our office to apply for the vacancies. I heard there were many applicants but Phillips and I were lucky enough to be selected, and one Frank Whyte, an assistant professor of engineering from St Andrew's University.

I think it was fortunate for me that I was called in next after Phillips, for I gathered from the Board that the work at Workington would, in their opinion, afford exactly the experience they were looking for, and instead of trying to find out what sort of experience I had had they proceeded to describe the work and then to inquire if that was so and if I had been associated with it. I often felt that I owed my selection to the fact that Phillips's interview had preceded mine. Be that as it may, we were as I have said, both selected, together with Frank Whyte. Next came the medical examination and I feel it was somewhat ironic that Phillips should be turned down. I heard later that he had, before very long, obtained an appointment with ICI. So perhaps, after all, it was just as well for him that he had failed the medical test.

So now here I was setting out once more on a new adventure. Wasn't it well, I thought, that I had staked everything on gaining a qualification. I felt I needed that what Burns calls 'the guinea stamp' to enable me to carve out a niche for myself 'in the world's field of battle'.

Captain David Campbell worked as an engineer for the Calcutta Port Commissioners during the construction of the King George's Dock, Calcutta. On his return to Ireland he was appointed Resident Architect for the construction of the Irish War Memorial in Dublin. In 1938 he became the Resident Engineer for the Construction of Shannon Airport, and later for the construction of concrete runways at Dublin Airport, and finally at the Dublin military airport, Baldonnel from where he retired. He died on 10 April 1971 aged eighty-three years.